GAS GRIDDLE
COOKBOOK

By James Stone

Table
of content

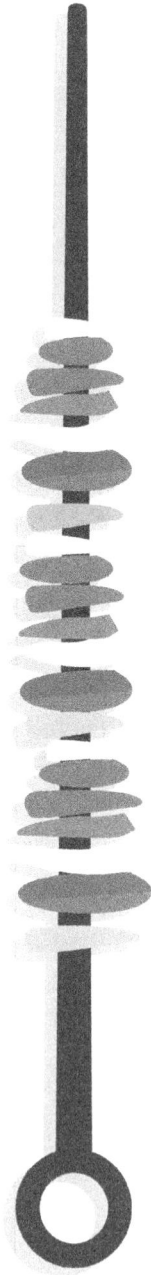

Chapter 5 .... **69**

Chapter 6 .... **81**

Turkey Recipes

Chapter 7

Pork Recipes

Chapter 8 106

Beef Recipes 106

High-Low Strip Steak 107

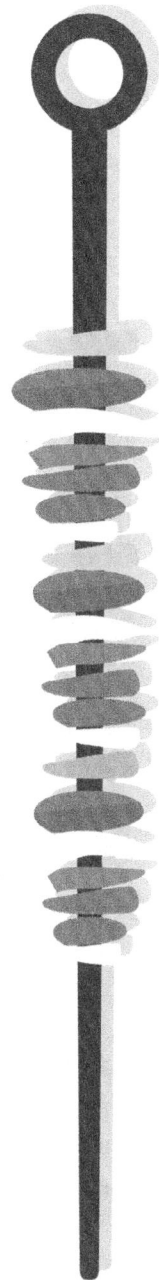

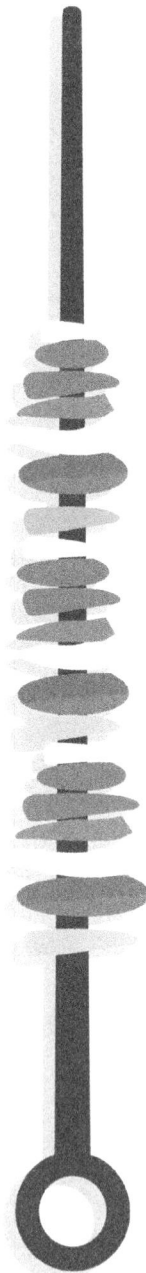

Introduction

The aroma of meat wafting through the air and the feeling of being surrounded by friends and family creates a memorable event: many wonderful memories are created during celebrations and gatherings that feature outdoor griddles and barbeques.

I wrote this cookbook to help you make the most of those memories and feed your pals the most delicious meal they've ever had, making them talk about it for years.

After all, nothing beats a hearty barbecue while the sun is directly overhead. That buffalo-sauced meaty goodness, glistening with melted butter and cheese... It takes an insane person not to seek this sensation on the palate.

But enough with the daydreaming: let's get started!

Chapter 1:
What Is An Outdoor Gas Griddle?

GAS GRILL

This even-heating appliance cooks up to four people at once while locking in the heat of your stove-top and producing seared edges. It's similar to grilling or cooking with one very large pan, making it ideal for simple and quick dishes.

The versatility of these griddles makes them one of our favorite kitchenware items. They may be used to bake a cake, cook pancakes and fry bacon! They are composed of cast iron and have chrome plating which helps them to hold heat and makes them the perfect surface for searing steaks. They are also really simple to store because you can fold them flat.

Components Of Outdoor Gas Griddlers

IGNITERS

These small parts pack a punch, designed to make lighting your gas griddle easier. Igniters use electricity to generate a spark, igniting the gas flowing through the burner tubes. Older model gas griddles do not have igniters, so you must reach inside the griddle with a lighter wand or long match. Igniters usually fail due to corroded wire connections and are often the first component to fail on an outdoor gas griddle. Repairing is simple: swap out the bad igniter module for a new one. Ensure that the part is specific to the brand and type of griddle you own.

BURNER TUBES

These look like long cylinders of perforated metal. When the gas griddle is in operation, the gas flows through the tubes and out of the holes where it burns, creating the heat that cooks the food on the griddle. The most common way for burner tubes to go bad is corrosion. If the rusted tubes are not replaced in time, they can cause large rust holes, allowing too much gas to flow through some spots and not enough in others. The corroded tubes must be removed, and new tubes must be put in place and connected to the gas supply manifold.

MANIFOLD

Griddle manifolds are what connect the gas supply to the burner tubes. They are usually installed on the front of a gas griddle, underneath the burner control knobs and protective cover. Manifolds are susceptible to corrosion over time, like the other components mentioned above. When this happens, they stop transporting gas properly to the burner tubes. To replace the manifold, remove the control knobs, and cover and disconnect the old one from the burner tubes and gas line. Slide the new manifold into place and make sure everything is connected again.

REGULATOR

Regulators connect propane tanks to the outdoor gas griddle, and it reduces the gas before it reaches the burner tubes. Faulty regulators sometimes let gas leak out before reaching the griddle or stop the gas flow altogether. When replacing the regulator, disconnect the old one from the propane tank and gas line and reconnect everything to the new one. A quick test to check if everything is in order is to spray a mixture of water and dish soap on all the connections before turning the gas on. You will know if there is a leak when the soapy solution bubbles continuously.

Tools And Accessories

INFRARED AND PROBE THERMOMETER

When preparing food to your specifications, it is crucial to accurately read the temperature of food, surfaces, and equipment such as the griddles.

For example, obtaining a rapid and accurate reading of your griddle temperature is the best method to ensure that your porterhouse steak is served at 130°F for the ideal medium-rare.

Infrared thermometers are fast, easy to use, and provide more precise temperature readings than other methods. This thermometer allows you to "point and shoot" to determine the griddle surface temperature (normally shown through a small LCD screen), so depending on the food you want to cook, you'll know if the griddle is ready. After this, you can use the collapsible review to determine the core temperature of the food while cooking. The last recorded temperature can also be frozen for quick reference in most Infrared And Probe Thermometers.

You will no longer have to "hope the food is done" or be nauseated when cutting into your steak. With this handy tool, you can eliminate the guesswork from your cooking.

SPATULA

A spatula is a tool used to flip food while cooking and it is typically made of metal that can withstand high heat. Spatulas' different shapes, sizes, and materials vary in their use and effectiveness. Spatulas come in different types and are designed for different purposes, but one thing they have in common is that they are designed to turn food over while cooking by lifting it from the surface. Spatulas with larger curved ends with deep indentations also make flipping foods easier because there is less friction between the sides of the flipped food than surfaces without indentations.

BENCH SCRAPER

Bench scrapers are handy, especially when cooking outdoors at your campsite. A bench scraper will easily scrape excess grease off your griddle, making cleaning up a breeze and allowing you to return to more important tasks on the trip.

CARRYING TRAY

Most outdoor gas griddles have one novel yet vital element that needs to be observed when using the device. That is a carrying tray. When used with the griddle, it will prevent liquid spills from making their way onto valuable surfaces around your griddle. The carrying tray also helps circulate air and create a more consistent cooking surface for your food on the griddle. This equipment will help reduce frustration and ensure you don't burn or overcook one item during your mealtime preparation chores (especially during camping).

GRIDDLE COVER

A grill cover protects your grill's mechanism and components from the elements, particularly precipitation. Several metal components on your grill might rust if not kept dry (at least for the most part).

Similarly, a grill cover can keep your grill looking and feeling good. If you store your grill in direct sunshine, a cover may protect the knobs and handles from becoming too hot, making it simpler to begin cooking.

Additionally, it helps safeguard your barbecue against additional animal contaminants, such as bird excrement and nests.

If you maintain your griddle correctly, it will continue functioning as if it were brand new, allowing you to prepare the best meals possible. A grill cover may significantly aid in this endeavor. Furthermore, you do not want your meals to be contaminated with dirt or pollen. Be careful to utilize a grill cover correctly if you want to do so. Otherwise, the aim would be somewhat defeated.

CHOPPER/SCRAPER

If there are stubborn stains and sticky foods on your griddle, a griddle scraper will greatly assist in cleaning it properly.

In addition to saving time, griddle scrapers are more efficient than scouring pads or spatulas. The thicker metal of a griddle scraper was designed to provide the operator additional force and leverage while scraping off stubborn food remains from a griddle top.

While cleaning a griddle without a griddle scraper is possible, you will be extremely grateful to have a decent griddle scraper when you meet difficult spots.

WATER SQUEEZE BOTTLE

Homeowners must have a portable water bottle or something for outdoor gas griddle cooking. These devices are easy to use and make clean-up easy, but they also ensure you always have water ready for your griddle.

What Are The Differences In Cooking With A Griddle And A Grill? Is It An Outdoor Griddle Better Than A Grill?

Grills and Griddles are cooking devices that aid in the grilling of food. Cooking food on a grill entails introducing it to direct heat. Both gas and electricity can be used as heat sources. However, there are some differences between the griddle and the grill.

While many true barbecue fans can tell the difference between a grill and a griddle, that isn't always true for newbies or those who do not want to barbeque frequently. Here are some significant differences to ensure you know what to opt for:

COOKING SURFACE

The most noticeable distinction between the two is the cooking surface that should be used to distinguish them.

A grill is made of cast iron grates or stainless steel or open spaces between them to let the oils and fats from the meal drain away in their most basic form. A bigger flat plate with elevated ridges is used in modern closed-design grills.

On the other hand, the griddle provides a flat, smooth cooking surface similar to a hotplate. The griddle and grill cooking surfaces are heated from underneath and can be powered by charcoal or electricity.

TYPICAL USES

On the griddle, you can cook nearly everything cooked on a grill, whereas the taste will be different.

Grills are frequently preferred for steaks, sandwiches, hamburgers, chops, and most vegetables. Grills are ideal for giving your food a smoky flavor and some great grill marks. However, if you use typical grills with open wires, you won't be able to cook items that start as liquids, such as pancakes.

On the other hand, the griddle is ideal for making everything from pancakes to bacon and sausages for breakfast. The griddle is versatile and can also make burgers, sear steaks, and cook anything normally cooked on a frying pan or hotplate.

COOKING TEMPERATURE

The cooking temperature is one of the primary differences between the grill and the griddle. And this will be one of the most important factors in deciding between the two.

A typical grill cooks at temperatures of 400 ° F, substantially higher than the 350 ° F that a griddle cooks at.

Furthermore, unlike the griddle, where there is a strong metal barrier between the two, the food will use greater temperatures if you use a typical open-style grill. This reduces the possibility of flare-ups and thus makes them safer to use.

IDEAL PLACE TO USE IT

In addition to producing a lot of heat, grills emit a lot of smoke when cooking making them ideal for outdoor cooking. On the other hand, many modern grills are designed primarily for indoor usage and have a more effective ventilation system.

On the other hand, the griddles do not generate much heat and aren't particularly smoky, so they may be used indoors and out.

In addition, the griddle's lower risk of flare-ups makes it better suited for indoor use, as there is very little to worry about when using one.

FOOD TEXTURE AND TASTE

Because these are two very different cooking processes, each food's texture, and flavor will be considerably different.

Grilled dishes will have a somewhat burnt flavor, charred texture, and appealing grill marks. This texture and flavor will be even more noticeable when using coal or charcoal-pellet-powered grills.

When cooked on a griddle, your meats, and other foods will always have a crispy outside layer, but they will not be as crispy as when cooked on a grill. However, because the foods rarely dry out, they will have a much softer center than when cooked on a grill. Food will smell and taste more like traditional roasted food because it will not contact an open flame.

EASE OF CLEANING

Cleaning your barbecuing appliance, as much as you may hate it, is a necessary part of ownership, so when deciding between the grill and the griddle, consider which one will be easiest to clean.

Compared to the grates on a standard grill, a griddle's smooth and flat surface will be considerably easier to clean. You have extra nooks and crannies with the grill, which can be difficult to reach and clean fully because they will hold on to some burnt fats.

Cleaning your griddle with warm water and a flat scraper is frequently required, but cleaning the grill will require a stiff brush, extra elbow grease, and more time.

BUYING AND OWNERSHIP COST

When deciding between the grill and the griddle, price is a crucial deciding factor, and you must analyze both the cost of purchasing both appliances and the ownership costs.

Grills are usually the least expensive, but the price will vary depending on the style, size, and fuel source. Furthermore, grills will be less expensive, particularly when utilizing simple charcoal versions, and hence will not have high ownership costs.

On the other hand, Griddles may be fairly costly to purchase, especially if you go for the more expensive and feature-rich model versions with a big cooking surface. However, they will never have high ownership costs unless you get a huge power-hungry electric model.

How Does It Work?

Smoking on an outdoor gas griddle may differ slightly from another smoker's, but it is not difficult. Below is the step-by-step on how to smoke using an outdoor gas griddle.

1. Turn on the outdoor gas griddle and heat it.

2. A sheet of aluminum foil should be used to cover the griddle.
   ◊   Depending on the amount of meat or vegetables you intend to smoke, you can either utilize a sheet of aluminum foil the same size as the griddle or a significantly smaller one.
3. Wrap a couple of bricks with aluminum foil and arrange them on the griddle, right on the aluminum foil.
   ◊   Give spaces between the wrapped bricks and spread wood chips in between the wrapped bricks.
4. Spread wood chips in between the wrapped bricks and create smoke.
5. Set a cooling rack on the wrapped bricks over the wood chips and put an aluminum pan on the cooling rack.
6. Place the seasoned meat or veggies in the aluminum pan, build a wall from aluminum foil around the cooling rack to centralize the smoke, and put another aluminum pan to cover the meat or veggies.
7. Start smoking. The smoke generated by the outdoor gas griddle will cook your meat perfectly, resulting in delicious smoked food that fulfills your expectation.

Undoubtedly, this is one of the ways smoking almost anyone can, even those with no experience.

Do not hesitate and ignite your outdoor gas griddle now!

Chapter 2
Breakfast Recipes

Crisp Bread Sticks

Ingredients Needed:

◊ 2 eggs
◊ 4 bread slices, cut each bread slice into 3 pieces vertically
◊ 2/3 cup of milk
◊ 1/4 ~tsp of ground cinnamon
◊ 1 ~tsp full of vanilla

**PREPARATION:
10 MINS**

**COOKING TIME:
10 MINS**

**SERVING
PORTIONS:
2**

Preparation Process:

1. Set the griddle to preheat at medium-low heat.
2. Whisk eggs, cinnamon, vanilla, and milk in a dish.
3. Grease the top of the griddle using cooking spray.
4. Immerse each piece of bread into the egg mixture, ensuring to coat it properly.
5. Set coated bread pieces on top of the hot griddle and allow to cook until golden brown on both sides.
6. Serve when ready!

Nutrition Values: Cals: 166 Fat: 7g Carbs: 14g Proteins: 10.4g

Lemon-Garlic Artichokes

Ingredients Needed:

◊ Juice of 1/2 lemon
◊ ½ cup of canola oil
◊ 3 garlic cloves, well minced
◊ Common salt/sea salt to taste
◊ Freshly ground black chili pepper to taste
◊ 2 large artichokes, trimmed and halved

PREPARATION:
15/30 MINS

COOKING TIME:
15 MINS

SERVING PORTIONS:
4 SLICES

Preparation Process:

1. Preheat the griddle to medium-high heat.
2. While the unit is preheating in a medium mixing bowl, combine the lemon juice, oil, and garlic. Season with common salt/sea salt and Chili pepper, and then brush the artichoke halves with the lemon-garlic mixture.
3. Place the artichokes on the griddle, cut side down. Gently press them down to maximize grill marks. Grill for 8 to 10 mins, occasionally basting generously with the lemon-garlic mixture throughout cooking until blistered on all sides.

Nutrition Values: Cals: 285 Fat: 28g Carbs: 10g Proteins: 3g

Sausage Scramble Vegetable

Ingredients Needed:

◊ 8 eggs, beaten
◊ ½ lb. sausage, well cut into thin rounds or well minced
◊ 1 green bell pepper, well cut
◊ 1 yellow onion, well cut
◊ 1 cup of white mushrooms, well cut
◊ 1 ~tsp full of common salt/sea salt
◊ ½ ~tsp of black Chili pepper
◊ Vegetable oil to taste

PREPARATION: 15 MINS

COOKING TIME: 20 MINS

SERVING PORTIONS: 4

Preparation Process:

1. Turn on the 4 burners of the griddle and turn their knobs to medium heat.
2. Let the griddle preheat for 5 mins.
3. Brush the griddle top with vegetable oil and add the Chili peppers and mushrooms.
4. Cook until browned and then add the onions.
5. Season by adding black Chili pepper and common salt/ sea salt and then let it cook until the onions are soft.
6. Add the sausage to the griddle and mix it with the vegetables. Cook until lightly browned.
7. Add the eggs and mix with the vegetables and then let it cook until the eggs reach the desired doneness.
8. Use a large spatula to remove the scramble from the griddle.
9. Serve.

Nutrition Values: Cals: 342 Fat: 24.9g Carbs: 6.3g Proteins: 23.2g

Easy Cheese Toast

Ingredients Needed:

◊ 2 bread slices
◊ 2 ~tsp full of butter
◊ 2 cheese slices

PREPARATION:
10 MINS

COOKING TIME:
10 MINS

SERVING PORTIONS:
1

Preparation Process:

1. Set the griddle to preheat at medium-low heat.
2. Top one bread slice with cheese slices and cover with another bread slice.
3. Smear butter on both sides of the bread slices.
4. Set sandwich on hot griddle top and allow to cook until cheese is melted and bread slices are golden brown.
5. Serve when ready!

Nutrition Values: Cals: 340 Fat: 26g Carbs: 9.8g Proteins: 15.4g

Sausage Mixed Grill

Ingredients Needed:

◊ 8 small bell peppers
◊ 2 heads of radicchio, well sliced into 6 wedges
◊ Canola oil for sprinkling
◊ Common salt/sea salt to taste
◊ 6 breakfast sausage links
◊ Grounded Freshly black Chili pepper
◊ 6 hot or sweet Italian sausage links

PREPARATION:
15-30 MINS

COOKING TIME:
22 MINS

SERVING PORTIONS:
4 SLICES

Preparation Process:

1. Preheat the griddle to medium-high heat.
2. Brush the bell peppers and radicchio with the oil. Season with common salt/ sea salt and black Chili pepper.
3. Place the bell peppers and radicchio on the griddle and cook for 10 mins, without flipping.
4. Meanwhile, poke the sausages with a fork or knife and brush them with some of the oil.
5. After 10 mins, remove the vegetables and set them aside. Decrease the heat to medium. Place the sausages on the griddle and cook for 6 mins.
6. Flip the sausages and cook for 6 mins more. Remove the sausages from the grill.
7. Serve the sausages and vegetables on a large cutting board or serving tray.

Nutrition Values: Cals: 473 Fat: 34g Carbs: 14g Proteins: 28g

Almond Griddle Cakes

Ingredients Needed:

◊ 1 egg
◊ 1/2 cup of almond flour
◊ 1/2 ~tsp of baking powder
◊ 1/2 ~tbsp of heavy whipping cream
◊ 1 and 1/2 ~tbsp of Swerve

Preparation Process:

1. Set the griddle to preheat at medium-low heat.
2. Combine baking powder, almond flour, sweetener, and common salt/ sea salt in a dish.
3. Whisk the egg and heavy whipping cream in another mixing bowl.
4. Mix dry Ingredients with the wet ensuring to mix properly.
5. Grease the griddle top with cooking spray.
6. Place the dough on top of the hot griddle.
7. Allow pancakes to cook on both sides until lightly golden brown.
8. Serve when ready!

Nutrition Values: Cals: 90 Fat: 7g Carbs: 13g Proteins: 4g

Quick Banana Griddlecake

Ingredients Needed:

◊ 2 eggs
◊ 2 -tbsp full of vanilla Proteins: powder
◊ 1 large banana, mashed
◊ 1/8 -tsp of baking powder

PREPARATION:
10 MINS

COOKING TIME:
10 MINS

SERVING PORTIONS:
B

Preparation Process:

1. Set the griddle to preheat at medium-low heat.
2. Add all ingredients into a dish and combine thoroughly.
3. Grease the top of the griddle with cooking spray.
4. Spoon 3 -tbsp full of the batter on top of the hot griddle to make a pancake.
5. Allow cooking until lightly browned on both sides.
6. Serve when ready!

Nutrition Values: Cals: 79 Fat: 1.6g Carbs: 5.5g Proteins: 11g

Scallion Cauliflower Pancakes

Ingredients Needed:

◊ 2 eggs
◊ 1 -tbsp full of flax meal
◊ ½ cup of scallions, well cut
◊ ½ cauliflower head, grated
◊ ½ -tsp of Chili pepper
◊ 1 and ½ -tsp of common salt/sea salt

PREPARATION:
15 MINS

COOKING TIME:
10 MINS

SERVING PORTIONS:
3

Preparation Process:

1. Add grated cauliflower and 1 -tsp full of common salt/sea salt in a suitable mixing bowl and mix well. Set aside for 20 mins.
2. After 20 mins squeeze out all liquid from the cauliflower.
3. Add squeezed cauliflower into a suitable mixing bowl.
4. Add the rest of the recipe's Ingredients and mix well.
5. Grease the cooking surface of the griddle with cooking spray.
6. Turn on the 4 burners and turn their knobs to medium heat.
7. Let the griddle preheat for 5 mins.
8. Add a spoonful of cauliflower mixture on preheated griddle top and flatten out into small pancakes.
9. Cook the pancake for almost 2-3 mins on each side.
10. Serve.

Nutrition Values: Cals: 197 Fat: 17.9g Carbs: 5.2g Proteins: 5.9g

Tomato Omelet

Ingredients Needed:

◊ 2 eggs, lightly beaten
◊ 2 -tbsp full of fresh basil, well minced
◊ 1 -tbsp full of olive oil
◊ 1/2 tomato, well minced
◊ Chili Pepper to taste
◊ Common salt/sea salt to taste

PREPARATION:
10 MINS

COOKING TIME:
5 MINS

SERVING PORTIONS:
2

Preparation Process:

1. Set griddle to preheat at medium heat.
2. Pour some oil on the griddle top.
3. Place tomatoes on the griddle and cook until softened.
4. In a mixing bowl, mix the eggs with basil, Chili pepper, and common salt/ sea salt.
5. Turn the egg mixture on the tomato top and allow to cook until the eggs are done.
6. Serve when ready!

Nutrition Values: Cals: 125 Fat: 12g Carbs: 1g Proteins: 5.8g

Butter Almond Cauliflower Patties

Ingredients Needed:

◊ 2 eggs
◊ 1 large head cauliflower, cut into florets
◊ 1 ~tbsp full of butter
◊ ½ ~tsp of turmeric
◊ 1 ~tbsp full of nutritional yeast
◊ 2/3 cup of almond flour
◊ ¼ ~tsp of black Chili pepper
◊ ½ ~tsp of common salt/sea salt

PREPARATION:
10 MINS

COOKING TIME:
15 MINS

SERVING PORTIONS:
6

Preparation Process:

1. In a big saucepan, place cauliflower florets.
2. Cover the cauliflower florets with enough water to cover them.
3. Allow 8~10 mins for the water to boil.
4. Preheat the griddle by turning all its knobs to medium heat setting.
5. Grease the griddle top with butter.
6. Drain cauliflower thoroughly and add to a food processor then blend.
7. Place cauliflower rice in a suitable mixing bowl.
8. Toss in the remaining ingredients, excluding the butter, and whisk to incorporate.
9. Form small patties from the cauliflower mixture and cook for 3~4 mins per side on the hot griddle top.
10. Serve and enjoy.

Nutrition Values: Cals: 107 Fat: 6g Carbs: 9.9g Proteins: 6.6g

Kale Omelet with Parmesan Cheese

Ingredients Needed:

◊ 4 eggs
◊ 4 cups kale, well minced
◊ 1 ~tbsp full of Fresh sage, well minced
◊ 1/3 cup of parmesan cheese, grated
◊ ½ ~tsp full of Chili pepper
◊ ½ ~tsp full of common salt/sea salt

PREPARATION:
15 MINS

COOKING TIME:
15 MINS

SERVING PORTIONS:
3

Preparation Process:

1. Grease the cooking surface of the griddle with cooking spray.
2. Turn on the 4 burners and turn their knobs to medium heat.
3. Let the griddle preheat for 5 mins.
4. Add kale on preheated griddle top and then let it cook for mins or until wilted.
5. Beat eggs with sage, cheese, black Chili pepper and common salt/sea salt in a suitable mixing bowl.
6. Pour this egg mixture over the kale leaves and mix well.
7. Cook for almost 2 and ½ mins per side.
8. Serve.

Nutrition Values: Cals: 338 Fat: 12g Carbs: 14g Proteins: 27g

Cauliflower Fritters

Ingredients Needed:

◊ 2 eggs
◊ 1 large head cauliflower, cut into florets
◊ 1 ~tbsp full of butter
◊ ½ ~tsp of turmeric
◊ 1 ~tbsp full of nutritional yeast
◊ 2/3 cup of almond flour
◊ ¼ ~tsp of black Chili pepper
◊ ½ ~tsp of common salt/sea salt
◊ Water enough to cover cauliflower florets

PREPARATION:
15–30 MINS

COOKING TIME:
15 MINS

SERVING PORTIONS:
6

Preparation Process:

1. Add the cauliflower florets to a large pot.
2. Pour enough water to cover the cauliflower florets. Bring to boil for 8–10 mins.
3. Drain cauliflower well and transfer it to a food processor and process until it looks like rice.
4. Transfer cauliflower rice to a large mixing bowl.
5. Add the remaining ingredients except for butter to the mixing bowl and stir to combine.
6. Preheat the griddle to medium heat.
7. Melt butter on the hot griddle top.
8. Make small patties from the cauliflower mixture and place them on the hot griddle top and cook for 3–4 mins on each side or until lightly golden brown.
9. Serve when ready!

Nutrition Values: Cals: 155 Fat: 10g Carbs: 11.1g Sugar: 3.9g Proteins: 8.1g

Chapter 3
Burger Recipes

Dijon Salmon Burgers

Ingredients Needed:

◊ ½ pounds salmon fillet, skin and any remaining pin bones removed, cut into chunks
◊ 2 -tsp full of Dijon mustard
◊ 3 scallions, trimmed and well minced
◊ ¼ cup of breadcrumbs (preferably fresh)
◊ Common salt/sea salt and Chili pepper to taste
◊ Good-quality olive oil for brushing
◊ sesame hamburger buns or 8–10 slider buns (like potato or dinner rolls)
◊ 1 large tomato, cut into 4 thick slices

PREPARATION:
5 MINS

COOKING TIME:
11 MINS

SERVING PORTIONS:
4

Preparation Process:

1. Put about one quarter of the salmon and the mustard in a food processor and purée into a paste. Add the rest of the salmon and pulse until well minced.
2. Transfer to a mixing bowl, add the scallions, breadcrumbs, and a sprinkle of common salt/sea salt and Chili pepper. Mix gently just enough to combine. Form into 4 burgers ¾ to 1 inch thick.
3. Transfer to a plate, cover with plastic wrap, and chill until firm, at least 2 or up to 8 hours.
4. Turn the control knob to the high position, when the griddle is hot, brush the burgers with oil on both sides, then put them on the griddle. Cook for 11 mins.
5. After 11 mins, check the burgers for doneness. Cooking is complete when the internal temperature reaches at least 165 degrees F on a food thermometer.
6. If necessary, close the hood and continue cooking for up to 2 mins more.
7. Remove the burgers from the griddle. Put the buns on the griddle, cut side down, and toast for 1 to 2 mins.
8. Serve the burgers on the buns, topped with the tomato if using.

Nutrition Values: Cals: 123 Fat: 21g Proteins: 16g Fiber:12g

Spiced Lamb Burger with Cucumber

Ingredients Needed:

◊ ¼ pounds lean ground lamb
◊ Ground cumin to taste
◊ ¼ -tsp of ground cinnamon
◊ ½ -tsp of common salt/sea salt
◊ ½ -tsp of freshly ground black Chili pepper
◊ whole wheat pitas
◊ ½ medium cucumber, peeled and well cut
◊ ½ cup of simple Garlic Yogurt Sauce

PREPARATION:
5 MINS

COOKING TIME:
5 MINS

SERVING PORTIONS:
4

Preparation Process:

1. Put the lamb in a medium mixing bowl with the cumin, cinnamon, common salt/sea salt, and Chili pepper. Using a fork, mix the seasonings into the meat and then, with your hands, form the mixture into 4 patties, each about 1 inch thick.
2. Turn the control knob to the high position, when the griddle is hot place the burgers and cook for 5 mins without flipping.
3. Remove the burgers and cover them to keep them warm. Put a burger into each pita, stuff a few cucumber slices in there too, and spoon some of the yogurt sauce over the top.
4. Serve immediately.

Nutrition Values: Cals: 354 Fat: 21g Proteins:36g

Classic Tex-Mex Turkey Burgers

Ingredients Needed:

◊ 1/3 cup of finely crushed corn tortilla chips
◊ 1 egg beaten
◊ ¼ cup of salsa
◊ 1/3 cup of shredded Chili pepper Jack cheese
◊ A pinch of common salt/sea salt
◊ Freshly ground black Chili pepper to taste
◊ 1 pound ground turkey
◊ 1 -tbsp full of olive oil
◊ 1 -tsp full of paprika

PREPARATION: 10 MINS

COOKING TIME: 15 MINS

SERVING PORTIONS: 4

Preparation Process:

1. In a medium mixing bowl, combine the tortilla chips, egg salsa, cheese, common salt/ sea salt, and Chili pepper, and mix well.
2. Add the turkey and mix gently but thoroughly with clean hands.
3. Form the meat mixture into patties about ½ inch thick. Make an indentation in the center of each patty with your thumb so the burgers don't puff up while cooking.
4. Brush the patties on both sides with olive oil and sprinkle with paprika.
5. Turn the control knob to the high position. When the griddle is hot, griddle for 14 to 16 mins or until the meat registers at least 165 degrees F.
6. Serve and enjoy!

Nutrition Values: Cals: 354 Fat: 21g Proteins: 36g

Teriyaki Beef Burgers

Ingredients Needed:

◊ 1¼ pounds lean ground beef
◊ 1 small onion, well minced
◊ ¼ cup of teriyaki sauce
◊ 3 ~tbsp full of Italian-flavored breadcrumbs
◊ 2 ~tbsp full of grated Parmesan cheese
◊ 1 ~tsp full of common salt/ sea salt
◊ 1 ~tsp full of freshly ground black Chili pepper
◊ 3 ~tbsp full of sweet pickle relish
◊ 4 Kaiser rolls, toasted

PREPARATION:
5 MINS

COOKING TIME:
4 MINS

SERVING PORTIONS:
4

Preparation Process:

1. Place the meat, onion, teriyaki sauce, breadcrumbs, Parmesan cheese, common salt/ sea salt, and Chili pepper in a medium mixing bowl.
2. The meat should be mixed with the ingredients using a fork before being formed into 4 patties that are each about 1 inch thick.
3. Heat the griddle up very quickly. Place the burgers on the heated griddle and cook for 4 mins without turning.
4. Take out the burgers and cover them to maintain warmth. Before placing each burger inside a bun, add a spoonful of sweet pickle relishes on top.
5. Serve right away.

Nutrition Values: Cals: 519 Fat: 23g Proteins: 33g

BBQ Pineapple Turkey Burgers

Ingredients Needed:

◊ 1 -tsp full of BBQ rub
◊ 1 can of well-cut pineapple
◊ 4 slices Swiss cheese
◊ 1 cup of fresh raw spinach, stems removed
◊ 4 sets of hamburger buns Patty
◊ 1 lb. ground turkey
◊ ½ cup of breadcrumbs
◊ ¼ cup of teriyaki sauce
◊ 1 small yellow onion, well diced
◊ 2 -tbsp full of. finely well-minced parsley
◊ 2 garlic cloves, well minced
◊ 1 egg beaten

PREPARATION:
5 MINS

COOKING TIME:
9 MINS

SERVING PORTIONS:
4

Preparation Process:

1. Place all of the patty ingredients in a large mixing bowl and thoroughly stir by hand.
2. Split the mixture evenly into four portions. Lay the four parts on parchment paper after forming them into patties. Apply BBQ rub evenly to each patty. Put for 30 mins in the refrigerator.
3. Heat the griddle to a high temperature. Place the hamburgers and pineapple pieces on the hot griddle.
4. Cook without turning for four mins. Burgers are removed and covered to maintain warmth.
5. After the burgers have been turned over, top each patty with a slice of Swiss cheese and let it melt while the burgers cook through. Take off the griddle.
6. Place burgers, spinach, and pineapple on buns and serve.

Nutrition Values: Cals: 554 Fat: 11g Proteins: 26g

Authentic New Mexican Salsa Verde

Ingredients Needed:

◊ Garlic, as required (Unpeeled)
◊ A tiny bamboo skewer or wooden toothpick
◊ 1 cup of roasted Anaheim or New Mexican green chiles, well sliced into 1/4-inch strips (8 to 10 chilies).
◊ 2 ~tbsp full of well minced fresh cilantro
◊ 2 ~tsp full of fresh lime juice, or more to taste
◊ ½ ~tsp of ground cumin
◊ ½ ~tsp of dried oregano
◊ Coarse (kosher or common salt/ sea salt)
◊ Fresh black Chili pepper

PREPARATION: 5 MINS

COOKING TIME: 15 MINS

SERVING PORTIONS: 1 CUP

Preparation Process:

1. Turn the griddle's heat to high. When ready to cook, spray the griddle with a little oil.
2. Put the burgers on the hot griddle in step two. The burgers will be finished after 4 to 6 mins of grilling.
3. Place the garlic cloves and cook them for 2 to 3 mins per side, until they are soft and gently browned (4 to 6 mins in all). Scrape off any very burned garlic peel.
4. In a blender, combine the garlic, chile strips, cilantro, lime juice, cumin, and oregano. Purée until smooth, brushing off the sides of the blender as necessary.
5. Place the pot over medium heat and gently simmer the salsa. Stirring occasionally with a wooden spoon, let simmer for 5 to 8 mins or until thick and flavorful.
6. The salsa should be thick but pourable (around the consistency of heavy cream); if additional water is required, add it. The salsa should be well-seasoned; if extra lime juice is required, add it along with common salt/ sea salt and Chili pepper to taste.

Nutrition Values: Cals: 214 Fat: 16g Proteins: 36g Fiber: 2g

Worcestershire Bruch Burgers

Ingredients Needed:

◊ ¼ cup of light sour cream
◊ 5 ~tbsp full of white horseradish
◊ ¼ ~tsp full of common salt/ sea salt
◊ 1¼ pounds lean ground beef
◊ ¼ cup of tomato sauce
◊ 2 ~tbsp full of Worcestershire sauce
◊ A dash or 2 of hot sauce
◊ 1 ~tsp full of celery common salt/sea salt
◊ 4 beefsteak tomato slices
◊ 4 brioche buns or hamburger buns, toasted
◊ 2 celery stalks, with leafy greens, each cut into 4 pieces

PREPARATION:
5 MINS

COOKING TIME:
5 MINS

SERVING PORTIONS:
4

Preparation Process:

1. Combine the sour cream, common salt/sea salt, and 2 ~tbsp of horseradish in a small mixing bowl.
2. Add the remaining 3 ~tbsp of horseradish, tomato sauce, Worcestershire sauce, spicy sauce, and celery common salt/ sea salt to the beef in a medium mixing bowl.
3. Combine the meat and seasonings with a fork, and then, using your hands, shape the mixture into four patties, each of which should be approximately an inch thick.
4. When the griddle is heated, turn the control to the high setting add the hamburgers, and cook for 4 mins without turning.
5. Burgers are removed and covered to maintain warmth. Sandwich between toasted bread and top with a ~tbsp full of horseradish sour cream and a tomato slice.
6. Serve immediately with the celery sticks.

Nutrition Values: Cals: 447 Fat: 27g Proteins: 35g

Cheddar Chipotle Burgers

Ingredients Needed:

◊ 1 and ¼ pounds of lean ground beef
◊ 2 ~tbsp full of chipotle puree
◊ ½ ~tsp of common salt/sea salt
◊ ¼ ~tsp of freshly ground black Chili pepper
◊ 4 ounces of sliced cheddar cheese
◊ 1 avocado, halved, pitted, and well cut
◊ ¼ head iceberg lettuce, shredded
◊ 4 hamburger buns, toasted

PREPARATION:
5 MINS

COOKING TIME:
15 MINS

SERVING PORTIONS:
4

Preparation Process:

1. Add the common salt/ sea salt, Chili pepper, and chipotle purée to the meat in a medium mixing bowl. Mix the seasonings into the meat with a fork before using your hands to shape the mixture into 4 patties that are each about 1 inch thick.
2. When the griddle is heated, turn the control knob to the high setting add the burgers, and cook for 4 mins without flipping.
3. Add a slice of cheese to the top of each burger and cook for an additional minute, or until the cheese melts. Burgers are removed and covered to maintain warmth.
4. Before placing each burger between a bun, top it with a couple of slices of avocado and some shredded lettuce.
5. To make the chipotle puree, add the liquid from the canned chipotles to a blender or food processor and mix until smooth.
6. The puree can be stored in the refrigerator for up to two weeks by covering it with plastic wrap. A little of this stuff goes a long way because it is really hot.
7. Mix it into dips and marinades for meat. Several grocery stores sell the puree under an ethnic brand.
8. Serve.

Nutrition Values: Cals: 590 Fat: 38g Proteins: 37g

Mayo Poultry Burgers

Ingredients Needed:

◊ ¼ cup of mayonnaise
◊ 2 cloves garlic, 1 well minced, 1 peeled and left whole
◊ 2 oil-packed anchovy fillets, drained and mashed
◊ 2 ~tbsp full of freshly grated Parmesan cheese
◊ 1 ~tbsp full of fresh lemon juice
◊ ½ ~tsp of Worcestershire sauce
◊ 1½ pounds of ground chicken or turkey
◊ Good-quality vegetable oil for oiling the grates
◊ ciabatta rolls, split into halves, or 8–10 slider buns
◊ Good-quality olive oil for brushing the rolls
◊ 4 leaves heart of romaine, trimmed

PREPARATION:
5 MINS

COOKING TIME:
15 MINS

SERVING PORTIONS:
4

Preparation Process:

1. Use wax paper to cover a baking sheet. In a small mixing bowl, combine the mayonnaise, well-minced garlic, anchovies, Parmesan, lemon juice, and Worcestershire; whisk until combined.
2. Add the chicken and 2 ~tbsp of the dressing to a medium mixing bowl. The remaining dressing should be covered and kept cold. Gently but thoroughly rub the dressing into the chicken with your hands.
3. Make 4 burgers out of the mixture that is between 3/4 and 1 inch thick. Place them on the prepared pan, cover them, and chill for at least an hour to firm them up.
4. When the griddle is heated, turn the control knob to the high setting and brush the cut sides of the rolls with olive oil. Place the burgers on the griddle after brushing them with oil on both sides.
5. Cook for 5 to 7 mins on each side, carefully rotating once with two spatulas, until golden on the outside and no longer pink in the center.
6. Toast the buns on the griddle with the sliced side down for the final couple of mins. When ready to serve, rub the entire garlic clove on the cut side of the top of each roll.
7. Arrange a burger on the bottom half of the roll, top it with a romaine leaf, a dollop of the remaining dressing and serve.

Nutrition Values: Cals: 200 Fat: 11g Proteins: 12g Fiber: 2g

Turkey Burger Patty Melts

Ingredients Needed:

◊ 2 pounds turkey burger patties, frozen, cooked and crumbled 1/4 cup of fat-free mayonnaise

◊ 2 ~tsp full of prepared horseradish

◊ 6 slices (about 1/4 inch thick) or 12 slices (1/8 inch thick) sourdough bread; toasted

PREPARATION: 15 MINS

COOKING TIME: 10 MINS

SERVING PORTIONS: 6

Preparation Process:

1. Combine onion, mustard, ketchup, mayonnaise, and horseradish in a large mixing bowl. Add crumbled hamburger patties and stir.

2. Place slices of bread on a surface. For each slice of bread, spoon 1/4 of the turkey mixture on top. Add cheese, then place the second slice of bread on top.

3. Bring a griddle to a temperature where a drop of water will bounce off of it when placed over medium heat.

4. Sandwiches should be cooked for 3 to 5 mins, rotating once, or until golden brown and the cheese has melted.

5. Serve hot right away.

Nutrition Values: Cals: 278 Fat: 9g Carbs: 16g Proteins: 23g

Lamb and Cucumber Burger

Ingredients Needed:

◊ ¼ pounds of lean ground lamb
◊ 1 -tbsp full of ground cumin
◊ ¼ -tsp of ground cinnamon
◊ ½ -tsp of common salt/sea salt
◊ ½ -tsp of freshly ground black Chili pepper
◊ whole wheat pitas
◊ ½ medium cucumber, peeled and well cut
◊ ½ cup of Simple Garlic Yogurt Sauce

PREPARATION:
5 MINS

COOKING TIME:
5 MINS

SERVING PORTIONS:
4

Preparation Process:

1. In a medium mixing bowl, combine the lamb, cumin, cinnamon, common salt/ sea salt, and black Chili pepper. Using your hands, shape the beef mixture into four 1-inch-thick patties after forking the seasonings into the flesh.
2. Place the patties on the griddle and grill for 5 mins over high heat without flipping.
3. Take out the hamburgers and keep them hot by covering them.
4. Add a burger, a few cucumber slices, and a dollop of the yogurt sauce on each pita.
5. Serve immediately.

Nutrition Values: Cals: 635 Fat: 23.7g Carbs: 11.1g Proteins: 89g

Garlicky Pork Burgers

Ingredients Needed:

◊ ½ ~tsp of common salt/sea salt
◊ ½ ~tsp of black Chili pepper
◊ 2 cloves garlic, well minced
◊ 2 hard rolls

PREPARATION:
5 MINS

COOKING TIME:
10 MINS

SERVING PORTIONS:
2

Preparation Process:

1. Pulse the beef, Chili pepper, common salt/ sea salt and garlic in a food processor until it is coarsely ground, yet not significantly finer than well minced. (When using pre-ground beef, combine it with the Chili pepper, common salt/ sea salt, and garlic in a mixing bowl and stir gently with your hands.)
2. With as little handling as possible, form the beef into four 1~ to 112-inch-thick patties to avoid crushing it. (This can be prepared in advance and kept chilled until you're about to griddle it.) The burgers should be cooked on the griddle for 10 mins without being turned; the core temperature should be 160°F.
3. Put food on a dish for serving.
4. Reheat the rolls in the oven.
5. Serve the patties on a slice of bread.

Nutrition Values: Cals: 154 Fat: 8g Carbs: 18.3g Proteins: 4.3g

Chapter 4
Vegetable And Side Dishes

Fire Roasted Salsa Recipe

Ingredients Needed:

◊ 5 tomatillos
◊ 5 beefsteaks or Roma tomatoes
◊ 1 red onion well cut in half
◊ 2 jalapeño Chili peppers
◊ Olive oil to taste
◊ 3 bell peppers capsicum, red, green, and yellow
◊ Kosher common salt/sea salt to taste
◊ 2 limes juiced
◊ 3 cloves garlic
◊ Round black Chili pepper to taste
◊ 1/4 cup of well minced cilantro coriander

PREPARATION:
20 MINS

COOKING TIME:
35 MINS

SERVING PORTIONS:
4

Preparation Process:

1. Preheat the griddle to the temperature of 375 to 400 degrees F. Mix the tomatoes, jalapenos, tomatillos, Chili peppers, onions, Chili pepper, common salt/ sea salt, and olive oil in a large mixing bowl and keep it aside.
2. Grill the vegetable whole for 10 to 15 mins.
3. Cut the tomatillos and tomatoes into large chunks.
4. Add Chili pepper and common salt/sea salt to taste.
5. Mix everything and leave for the flavors to infuse and serve when ready!

Nutrition Values: Cals: 172 Fat: 5g Carbs: 32g Proteins: 6g

Fried Cabbage

Ingredients Needed:

◊ 1 yellow onion well cut
◊ 1/2 green cabbage well cut
◊ beer as needed for cooking
◊ 4 slices thick bacon and large dice
◊ Common salt/sea salt and Chili pepper to taste

PREPARATION:
10 MINS

COOKING TIME:
25 MINS

SERVING PORTIONS:
4

Preparation Process:

1. Preheat a griddle to the temperature of medium-high heat.
2. Place onions, bacon, and cabbage on the griddle and cook it.
3. Usually, the onions will take 7 mins, the cabbage around 5 mins, and bacon around 10 mins.
4. Glaze with splashes of beer. Serve it with seasoning of Chili pepper and common salt/sea salt.

Nutrition Values: Cals: 87 Proteins: 2g Carbs: 12g

Grilled Potato Salad

Ingredients Needed:

◊ 1 lemon juiced
◊ 1 red onion finely well diced
◊ Common salt/sea salt to taste
◊ 1 ~tbsp full of olive oil
◊ 1 bunch of fresh dill finely well diced
◊ 2 pounds of potatoes

PREPARATION:
15 MINS

COOKING TIME:
45 MINS

SERVING PORTIONS:
4

Preparation Process:

1. Mix a pinch of the finely well-minced dill, onions, olive oil, lemon juice, and common salt/sea salt in a mixing bowl and keep it aside.
2. Preheat a griller to 600 degrees F temperature.
3. Clean the potatoes and dice them into even pieces.
4. Use a pot to boil the potatoes. After that, grill the potatoes to make them crispy.
5. Next, place the potatoes in the drill dressing and serve!

Nutrition Values: Cals: 225 Proteins: 5g Fat: 4g Carbs: 45g

Grilled Bacon Wrapped Asparagus

Ingredients Needed:

◊ Olive oil to taste
◊ 1 bunch of asparagus
◊ Blues Hog Bold and Beefy Seasoning or favorite beef rub
◊ 1/2 lemon juiced
◊ 1 packet of bacon

PREPARATION:
20 MINS

COOKING TIME:
40 MINS

SERVING PORTIONS:
6

Preparation Process:

1. Preheat the griddle to the temperature of 300 degrees F.
2. Wash the asparagus and cut it to the same size.
3. Mix Bold and Beefy Seasoning lemon juice, and olive oil along with the asparagus in a fresh mixing bowl.
4. Use one bacon to wrap four asparagus with the help of a toothpick.
5. Grill the asparagus and season with bold and beefy seasoning.
6. Serve when ready

Nutrition Values: Cals: 77 Proteins: 3g Carbs: 4g

Grilled Sweet Potatoes

Ingredients Needed:

◊ Olive oil to taste
◊ 1 sweet potato
◊ Freshly cracked black Chili pepper to taste
◊ Kosher common salt/sea salt to taste
◊ BBQ rub

PREPARATION:
10 MINS

COOKING TIME:
40 MINS

SERVING PORTIONS:
1

Preparation Process:

1. Cut the sweet potato into sixths or quarters based on its size.
2. Mix common salt/sea salt, Chili pepper, oil, and BBQ rub with sweet potato in a large mixing bowl.
3. Preheat the griddle or grill to the temperature of 400 degrees F. Grill the sweet potatoes for 20 to 30 mins and turn them in every 5 mins.
4. Remove the sweet potatoes from the grill and serve when ready!

Nutrition Values: Cals: 194 Proteins: 4g Fat: 1g Carbs: 45g

Grilled Herb Mushrooms

Ingredients Needed:

◊ 1/2 ~tbsp of toasted sesame oil
◊ 1 ~tbsp full of olive oil
◊ 2 ~tbsp full of soy sauce
◊ 1/4 cup of Shaoxing rice wine
◊ 1-inch ginger well minced
◊ 3 cloves garlic well minced
◊ 8 large mushrooms or 16 medium mushrooms
◊ 1/2 red Chili pepper finely well diced
◊ 2 sprigs of cilantro finely well diced

PREPARATION:
20 MINS

COOKING TIME:
30 MINS

SERVING PORTIONS:
8

Preparation Process:

1. Mix the toasted sesame oil, olive oil, soy sauce, Shaoxing rice wine, garlic, cilantro, ginger, and chili in a large mixing bowl.
2. Preheat the griddle or grill to the temperature of medium heat.
3. Grill the cleaned mushrooms until it gets grill marks for 5 to 10 mins.
4. Next, add 1 ~tsp full of the herb dressing to the mushrooms and cook for 10 to 15 mins.
5. Serve it with the mixed-in ingredients sauce.

Nutrition Values: Cals: 116 Fat: 6g Carbs: 9g Proteins: 5g

Grilled Bok Choy

Ingredients Needed:

◊ 2 baby bok choy
◊ 4 pats of butter
◊ 1 -tbsp full of herb rub to taste

PREPARATION:
5 MINS

COOKING TIME:
15 MINS

SERVING PORTIONS:
4

Preparation Process:

1. Preheat the grill or griddle to the temperature of medium heat.
2. Cut the bok choy into a two-piece and wash it properly.
3. Grill the cut side of the bok choy for 5 mins until it gets brown in color.
4. Flip the bok Choy and rub butter on the cut side.
5. When the bok choy leaves softened, then you can remove them from the grill.
6. Serve immediately.

Nutrition Values: Fat: 4g Cals: 46 Carbs: 2g Proteins: 1g

Grilled Baby Potato Salad

Ingredients Needed:

◇ 3 -tbsp full of lemon juice
◇ 1/4 cup of olive oil
◇ 2 -tbsp full of whole-grain mustard
◇ Blues Hog Bold and Beefy Seasoning
◇ 2 -tbsp full of white vinegar
◇ 6 slices of bacon
◇ 2 lb baby potatoes or tri-colored fingerlings
◇ 4 finely well cut green onions
◇ 1/4 cup of olive oil
◇ 1 sprig of parsley finely well diced

PREPARATION:
15 MINS

COOKING TIME:
35 MINS

SERVING PORTIONS:
8

Preparation Process:

1. Prepare salad dressing with lemon juice, vinegar, olive oil, mustard, and Blues Hog Bold and Beefy, and keep it aside.
2. Parboil the potatoes to make them soft.
3. Toss the thinly well-cut green onions, olive oil, and Blues Hog Bold and Beefy, and keep it aside.
4. Preheat the griddle or grill to the temperature of 300 degrees F.
5. Use the bacon to layer on the potatoes and grill until it cooks for 10 mins.
6. Serve it in a mixing bowl with the pre-made salad dressing.

Nutrition Values: Cals: 285 Fat: 20g Carbs: 22g Proteins: 5g

Grilled Romaine Salad

Ingredients

◊ 1/2 cup of extra virgin olive oil
◊ 1 clove of garlic, well minced or crushed
◊ 1/2 cup of balsamic vinegar
◊ Common salt/sea salt and Chili pepper, to taste
◊ 1 ~tsp full of ground mustard
◊ 1/4 lemon, juiced
◊ 1 head of romaine lettuce
◊ 1/2 cup of freshly grated Parmesan cheese
◊ 2 ~tsp full of garlic powder
◊ 2 ~tbsp full of olive oil

PREPARATION:
15 MINS

COOKING TIME:
16 MINS

SERVING PORTIONS:
2

Preparation Process:

1. Prepare the vinaigrette dressing with extra virgin olive oil, garlic, balsamic vinegar, common salt/sea salt, mustard, and Chili pepper, and keep it aside.
2. Preheat a griddle to the temperature of medium-high heat.
3. Remove the outer leaves from the romaine lettuce and slice it perfectly.
4. Mix the cheese, garlic powder, Chili pepper, and common salt/ sea salt in a fresh mixing bowl.
5. In another mixing bowl, mix lemon juice and oil.
6. Use the oil mixture on the lettuce and season with the cheese mixture.
7. Grill the lettuce for 40 sec, and it's ready.

Nutrition Values: Cals: 545 Proteins: 9g Carbs: 18g Fat: 48g

Grilled Corn and Peach Salsa

Ingredients Needed:

◊ 1 red bell pepper
◊ 4 ears of corn
◊ 1/2 medium red onion
◊ 1 habanero to personal preference
◊ 2 limes juiced about 3 -tbsp full of
◊ 2 large peaches
◊ Common salt/sea salt and Chili pepper to taste
◊ 1 -tbsp full of extra-virgin olive oil

PREPARATION:
25 MINS

COOKING TIME:
37 MINS

SERVING PORTIONS:
4

Preparation Process:

1. Rub the corn with oil, half the habanero, and quarter the bell pepper.
2. Heat a grill or griddle to the temperature of 400 degrees F.
3. Grill the red onion, corn, habanero, and bell pepper and let it cool.
4. Prepare the salsa ingredients corn kernels, habanero, red onion, and bell pepper.
5. Split the peaches in half and dice them into small pieces.
6. Gently mix the corn mixture, peach, olive oil, lime juice, Chili pepper, and common salt/ sea salt.

Nutrition Values: Cals: 177 Proteins: 5g Carbs: 34g Fat: 5g

Grilled Drunken Salsa Recipe

Ingredients Needed:

◊ 1 large red onion
◊ 4 large truss tomatoes
◊ 1 clove garlic
◊ 1 whole jalapeno seeded
◊ 1 -tbsp full of olive oil
◊ Common salt/sea salt and Chili pepper to taste
◊ 1/2 cup of cilantro well diced
◊ 1 can Indian Pale Ale beer

PREPARATION:
5 MINS

COOKING TIME:
5 MINS

SERVING PORTIONS:
4

Preparation Process:

1. Quarterly cut the onion and tomato. Season with Chili pepper and common salt/sea salt.
2. Preheat the griddle to medium temperature and grill onion, jalapeno, tomato, and garlic for 10 mins.
3. Blend the grilled onion, jalapeno, tomato, and garlic.
4. Use a skillet, add olive oil and add the blended tomato mixture to cook.
5. Next, add beer and cook for 10 mins.
6. After that, you can transfer the cooked stuff to a medium mixing bowl and serve it with the well diced cilantro.

Nutrition Values: Cals: 115 Fat: 4g Carbs: 13g Proteins: 2g

Grilled Eggplant Appetizer

Ingredients Needed:

◊ Olive oil for brushing eggplant and bell pepper
◊ 1 large red bell pepper
◊ 2 ~tbsp full of coarse common salt/sea salt
◊ 1 globe eggplant
◊ Balsamic reduction
◊ 1/2 cup of goat cheese softened
◊ Basil leaves for garnish

PREPARATION:
30 MINS

COOKING TIME:
1 HOUR

SERVING PORTIONS:
6

Preparation Process:

1. Preheat the griddle to medium-high heat temperature. Slice the eggplant into 1 cm or 3/8 inch.
2. Place it on the griddle and add olive oil and red Chili pepper.
3. Steam the bell pepper for half an hour and remove its skin.
4. Slice it into ¼ inch and keep it aside.
5. Sprinkle common salt/ sea salt on the cut eggplant from both sides.
6. Plate the eggplant with a basil leaf, 2 strips of bell pepper, and 1 ~tbsp full of goat cheese.

Nutrition Values: Cals: 100 Fat: 7g Carbs: 7g Proteins: 4g

Griddle Fried Rice

Ingredients

◊ 1 cup of shredded carrots
◊ 1/2-pound bacon well diced
◊ 1 red onion well diced
◊ 1 zucchini well diced
◊ 1 bunch of cilantros well minced
◊ 4 green onions, well cut
◊ 6 cups of cooked rice
◊ 1 to 2 jalapeños finely well diced
◊ Peanut oil, as needed
◊ Soy sauce to taste
◊ 6 eggs

PREPARATION: 15 MINS

COOKING TIME: 40 MINS

SERVING PORTIONS: 6

Preparation Process:

1. Preheat the griddle to medium-low temperature.
2. Add the well diced bacon and shredded carrots and let it grill.
3. After that, let it cool. Add the green onions, bacon oil, red onions, zucchini, and cilantro to the hot side. Add the jalapeño and mixture of bacon.
4. Add rice and soy sauce, then fry.
5. Mix all the other ingredients and cook them.
6. Next, add a little peanut oil and scrambled eggs and finish cooking.
7. Serve.

Nutrition Values: Cals: 476 Fat: 22g Carbs: 51g Proteins: 16g

Steak Scallops and Vegetables

Ingredients Needed:

◊ 2 cobs of corn
◊ 2 steaks
◊ 2 handfuls of green beans
◊ 1 -tbsp full of butter to taste
◊ 15 scallops
◊ Common salt/sea salt and Chili pepper to taste

PREPARATION:
5 MINS

COOKING TIME:
25 MINS

SERVING PORTIONS:
2

Preparation Process:

1. Preheat the griddle to medium heat. Grill the corn and add butter to melt.
2. Use a skillet and add green beans, steak, Chili pepper, and common salt/sea salt to cook.
3. Make sure all the vegetables are cooked in a proper way.
4. Add the scallops. Let it cool and serve it on a plate.

Nutrition Values: Cals: 706 Fat: 40g Carbs: 27g Proteins: 64g

Grilled Artichokes With Honey Dijon

Ingredients Needed:

◊ 6 whole artichokes
◊ ½ gallon water
◊ 3 ~tbsp full of Sea common salt/sea salt
◊ Olive oil to taste
◊ Common salt/sea salt to taste
◊ 1/4 cup of raw honey
◊ 1/4 cup of boiling water
◊ 3 ~tbsp full of Dijon mustard

PREPARATION:
15 MINS

COOKING TIME:
15 MINS

SERVING PORTIONS:
4

Preparation Process:

1. From top to bottom, cut the artichokes in half lengthwise.
2. Combine the 3 ~tbsp full of common salt/ sea salt and water. Before cooking soak the artichokes in the brine for 30 mins to several hours.
3. Preheat the griddle grill to medium-high heat.
4. Remove the artichokes from the brine, then sprinkle with olive oil and season with common salt/sea salt.
5. Griddle for 15 mins on each side, cut side down.
6. Reduce the heat to low and place the artichokes cut side down on the grill while you combine the honey, boiling water, and Dijon.
7. Brush the Dijon mixture over the cut side of the artichokes until completely absorbed.
8. Serve with protein of your choice, such as fish, steak, pig or chicken, or as a vegetarian option with rice or potatoes.

Nutrition Values: Cals: 601 Fat: 57g   Proteins: 8g Carbs: 21g

Easy Seared Green Beans

Ingredients Needed:

◊ 1 and 1/2 lbs green beans, trimmed
◊ 1 and 1/2 ~tbsp of rice vinegar
◊ 3 ~tbsp full of soy sauce
◊ 1 and 1/2 ~tbsp of sesame oil
◊ 2 ~tbsp full of sesame seeds, toasted
◊ 1 and 1/2 ~tbsp of brown sugar
◊ 1/4 ~tsp of black Chili pepper

PREPARATION:
15 MINS

COOKING TIME:
7 MINS

SERVING PORTIONS:
1

Preparation Process:

1. Cook for 3 mins in boiling water, then drain thoroughly.
2. Drain the green beans again and place them in iced water. Green beans should be patted dry.
3. Preheat the griddle on high.
4. Cooking oil should be added to the heated griddle top.
5. Stir in the green beans for 2 mins.
6. Stir in the soy sauce, brown sugar, vinegar, and Chili pepper for another 2 mins.
7. Toss in the sesame seeds to coat.
8. Serving immediately and enjoying

Nutrition Values: Cals: 100 Fat: 5g Carbs: 11.7g Sugar 3.9g Proteins: 3.1g

Smoked Butternut Squash

Ingredients Needed:

◊ 1 whole butternut squash
◊ 2 -tbsp full of olive oil
◊ 1 -tbsp full of brown sugar
◊ 1/2 -tbsp of chili powder
◊ 1 -tsp full of black Chili pepper
◊ 1 -tsp full of kosher common salt/sea salt
◊ 1/2 -tsp full of garlic powder

PREPARATION:
25 MINS

COOKING TIME:
120 MINS

SERVING PORTIONS:
1

Preparation Process:

1. Prep your smoker for 325 degrees Fahrenheit.
2. Using a knife, cut the squash in half lengthwise. Make the lines shown above on its skin.
3. Combine the olive oil, garlic powder, chili powder, and brown sugar in a mixing bowl. Brush the exposed top section with this mixture.
4. Place the butternut squash on the smoker for 1.5 hours, or until cooked to your liking. Brush the squash with the mixture again during the last 30 mins of smoking.
5. Take out the smoker and serve.

Nutrition Values: Cals: 110 Fat: 5.9g Carbs: 15.7g Proteins: 1.3g

Stir Fry Vegetables

Ingredients Needed:

◊ 2 medium potatoes, cut into small pieces
◊ 3 medium carrots, peeled and cut into small pieces
◊ 1/4 cup of olive oil
◊ 1 small rutabaga, peeled and cut into small pieces
◊ 2 medium parsnips, peeled and cut into small pieces
◊ Common salt/sea salt and Chili Pepper to taste

PREPARATION:
5 MINS

COOKING TIME:
5 MINS

SERVING PORTIONS:
1

Preparation Process:

1. Preheat the griddle on high.
2. Toss veggies with olive oil in a large mixing basin.
3. Transfer the veggies to the heated griddle top and stir fry until tender.
4. Serve immediately and enjoy.

Nutrition Values: Cals: 218 Fat: 12.8g Carbs: 25.2g Sugar 6.2g Proteins: 2.8g

Grilled Asparagus and Honey Glazed Carrots

Ingredients Needed:

◊ 1 bunch of asparagus, trimmed ends
◊ 1 lb. carrots, peeled
◊ 2 -tbsp full of olive oil
◊ Common salt/sea salt to taste
◊ 2 -tbsp full of honey
◊ Lemon zest

PREPARATION:
15 MINS

COOKING TIME:
50 MINS

SERVING PORTIONS:
2

Preparation Process:

1. Season the asparagus with common salt/ sea salt and Chili pepper. Drizzle honey and common salt/sea salt over the carrots.
2. Preheat the oven to 165°F for 15 mins with the lid closed.
3. Cook for 15 mins with the carrots in the sous vide. Cook for another 20 mins, or until the asparagus is tender.
4. Sprinkle the lemon zest over the carrots and asparagus.
5. Enjoy.

Nutrition Values: Cals: 1680 Fat: 30g Total Carbs: 10g Proteins: 4g

Grilled Corn With Soy Butter And Sesame

Ingredients Needed:

◊ 3 ~tbsp full of unsalted butter
◊ 1 scallion, both white and green parts, finely well minced
◊ 2 ~tbsp full of soy sauce
◊ 4 ears sweet corn, shucked and cut or broken in half crosswise
◊ 1 ~tbsp full of toasted sesame seeds

PREPARATION:
10 MINS

COOKING TIME:
12 MINS

SERVING PORTIONS:
2

Preparation Process:

1. In a saucepan over medium heat, melt the butter. Cook until the scallion loses its rawness, approximately 1 minute (you don't want the scallion to brown). Remove the pot from the heat and stir in the soy sauce.

2. Preheat the griddle grill to medium-high. Allow the griddle to heat until the oil shimmers but does not smoke.

3. Arrange the corn ears on the heated grill. Cook the corn for 2 to 3 mins on each side (8 to 12 mins total) until beautifully browned on both sides, basting with a little soy butter. Use a delicate touch while basting: you don't want to spill too much butter onto the grill.

4. Place the corn on a serving plate. Brush it with the remaining soy butter, sprinkle with sesame seeds, and serve when ready! immediately.

5. Place the sesame seeds in a dry cast-iron pan or equivalent heavy skillet to toast (do not use a nonstick skillet for this). Cook the sesame seeds until lightly toasted, approximately 3 mins, stirring the pan to ensure even toasting. Cool the roasted sesame seeds in a heatproof basin.

6. Serve when ready.

Nutrition Values: Cals: 44 Fat: 4g Proteins: 2g

Chapter 5
Poultry Recipes

Griddle Chicken Phillies

Ingredients Needed:

◊ 2 pounds chicken breasts, cut into thin strips
◊ 2 ~tbsp full of vegetable oil
◊ 2 onions, thinly well cut
◊ Common salt/sea salt and black Chili pepper, to taste
◊ 2 ~tbsp full of Worcestershire sauce
◊ 3 garlic cloves, well minced
◊ 12 provolone cheese slices
◊ 8 ounces of mushrooms, well cut
◊ 2 ~tbsp full of Old Bay Seasoning
◊ ½ cup of banana Chili peppers, well cut
◊ 6 hoagie buns
◊ ½ cup of mayo

PREPARATION:
10 MINS

COOKING TIME:
15 MINS

SERVING PORTIONS:
6

Preparation Process:

1. Warm the gas griddle to medium heat.
2. Brush the griddle with 1 ~tbsp full of vegetable oil.
3. Place the chicken on one side of the griddle and the onions and mushrooms on the other.
4. Season the chicken with common salt/ sea salt, Chili pepper, and Old Bay seasoning.
5. Cook for 8 mins, rotating and turning a few times and adding the Worcestershire sauce halfway through.
6. Next, combine the chicken, onions, and mushrooms.
7. Stir in the garlic and banana Chili peppers. Cook for an additional 8 mins, flipping and rotating once.
8. Toast the buns for 2 mins on the grill, cut side down.
9. Arrange the chicken and vegetables on the grill in six piles, then top each with two slices of provolone and turn off the grill.
10. Spread mayo on the hoagie buns and top with melted cheese.

Nutrition Values: Cals: 753 Fat: 39.2g Carbs: 34g Proteins: 64g

Chicken Fried Rice

Ingredients Needed:

◊ 1 cup of chicken breast
◊ ½ cup of bacon slices, well diced
◊ 1 cup of zucchini, well diced
◊ ½ cup of onion, well diced
◊ ½ cup f bell pepper, well diced
◊ 4 cups white long grain rice, fully cooked
◊ 1 -tbsp full of soy sauce
◊ 1/8 -tsp of Chili pepper
◊ 1 cup of white mushrooms, well diced.
◊ ½ cup of celery, well diced
◊ 1 large egg
◊ ¼ -tsp of common salt/ sea salt

PREPARATION:
10 MINS

COOKING TIME:
15 MINS

SERVING PORTIONS:
8

Preparation Process:

1. Heat the gas griddle for 10 mins on medium. Coat with oil.
2. Once the griddle is hot, add the well diced bacon and cook for about 5 mins or until the bacon begins to crisp.
3. Place the well diced chicken breast on a different portion of the griddle and season to taste. Cook the chicken until completely cooked but not overcooked.
4. Then, layer all the vegetables (zucchini, onion, celery, Chili peppers, and mushrooms) on top of the bacon. Add the bacon fat.
5. While the bacon, veggies, and chicken are cooking scramble one egg on a different part of the griddle (Ensure the griddle is greased first). Scramble the egg until just done.
6. Combine the bacon, vegetables, scrambled egg rice, common salt/ sea salt, and Chili pepper while still on the griddle.
7. Cook for a few mins while continuing to mix the ingredients together.
8. Add the chicken pieces to the rice mixture once they're fully cooked.

9. Drizzle roughly a ~tbsp full of soy sauce over the rice mixture and mix well. Cook until the desired level of doneness is reached.
10. Check the flavor of the chicken fried rice. If necessary, add extra soy sauce, common salt/ sea salt, and Chili pepper.
11. Remove from the griddle onto a serving dish once the appropriate flavor has been attained.
12. Enjoy.

Nutrition Values: Cals: 378 Fat: 1.8g Carbs: 76.4g Proteins: 11.1g

Marinated Chicken Breast

Ingredients Needed:

◊ 12 ounces of boneless, skinless chicken breasts
◊ 5 ounces of Italian dressing

PREPARATION:
10 MINS

COOKING TIME:
15 MINS

SERVING PORTIONS:
4

Preparation Process:

1. Carefully pierce the chicken breasts with a fork and place them in a sealable bag with the Italian dressing.
2. Keep the bag refrigerated for at least 12 hours, shaking it every 2 hours.
3. Turn the gas griddle to medium heat. Add some oil to the griddle.
4. When the griddle is hot, place the chicken breasts on it. Any leftover marinade should be discarded.
5. Cook for about 6 mins with the cover on.
6. Flip the chicken breasts and cook for an additional 7 mins.
7. When the chicken is thoroughly cooked, remove it from the griddle.

Nutrition Values: Cals: 265 Fat: 16.4g Carbs: 3.7g Proteins: 24.7g

Teriyaki Chicken Stir Fry

Ingredients Needed:

◊ 2 cups mixed veggies
◊ 4 chicken breasts, cut into chunks
◊ ½ cup of teriyaki sauce
◊ ¼ cup of olive oil

PREPARATION:
5 MINS

COOKING TIME:
15 MINS

SERVING PORTIONS:
4

Preparation Process:

1. Heat the gas griddle to medium heat, brush it with oil, and put the chicken pieces on it.
2. Cook the chicken for 2 mins, flipping halfway through. Push the chicken to one side of the griddle.
3. Brush a little oil on the opposite side of the griddle and toss in the vegetables.
4. Continue to cook the chicken and vegetables on various sides of the griddle at the same time, flipping often (around 8 mins).
5. Mix the chicken and vegetables on the griddle.
6. Pour in half of the teriyaki sauce and cook the meat and vegetables together, flipping regularly (about 1 minute). Pour in the remaining half of the sauce.
7. Dish out and serve.

Nutrition Values: Cals: 462 Fat: 23.7g Carbs: 14.3g Proteins: 46.1g

Griddle-Seared Chicken Breasts

Ingredients Needed:

◇ 2 chicken breasts
◇ Common salt/sea salt and black Chili pepper to taste
◇ 2 -tbsp full of white wine
◇ 2 -tbsp full of olive oil

PREPARATION:
5 MINS

COOKING TIME:
12 MINS

SERVING PORTIONS:
4

Preparation Process:

1. Season the chicken breasts with common salt/sea salt and black Chili pepper.
2. Heat up the gas griddle on low heat and drizzle olive oil over it.
3. Put the seasoned chicken on the griddle and cover it.
4. Cook for about 4 mins, uncover, then flip the breasts over.
5. Cover and cook for 4 more mins. Uncover and add the white wine.
6. Cook for another 4 mins and enjoy!

Nutrition Values: Cals: 205 Fat: 12.4g Carbs: 0.2g Proteins: 21.1g

Cheesy Chicken Quesadilla

Ingredients Needed:

◊ 8 ounces white mushrooms, well cut
◊ 1½ pounds chicken breast, well diced small
◊ ¾ cup of bell peppers, well diced small
◊ 6 (8-inch) soft taco wraps
◊ ½ -tsp of common salt/sea salt
◊ 1 -tbsp full of olive oil
◊ 2 cups of white onion, well cut
◊ 2 cups of Mexican blend cheese, shredded
◊ ¼ -tsp of Chili pepper

PREPARATION: 10 MINS

COOKING TIME: 10 MINS

SERVING PORTIONS: 6

Preparation Process:

1. Heat up the gas griddle to medium heat.
2. Brush a portion of the griddle with ½ -tbsp of olive oil.
3. Layer the vegetables in the hot oil.
4. Pour the remaining ½ -tbsp of olive oil over the griddle's other side.
5. Place the well diced chicken on top of the oil and season with common salt/sea salt and Chili pepper.
6. Cook until the vegetables are tender and the chicken is cooked through.
7. Mix the vegetables and cooked chicken on the griddle, then add 3 of the wraps.
8. Fill each wrap with a third of the vegetable and chicken mixture.
9. Sprinkle a third of the shredded cheese on top of each, then place another wrap on top of each.
10. Sauté one side of the chicken quesadilla, then flip it over and sauté until the cheese has melted.
11. Serve and enjoy.

Nutrition Values: Cals: 518 Fat: 31g Carbs: 20g Proteins: 39g

Griddled Turkey Reuben

Ingredients Needed:

◊ 4 slices of bread
◊ 4 slices turkey
◊ 4 slices Swiss cheese
◊ ½ cup of sauerkraut
◊ French dressing as required
◊ 2 -tbsp full of butter

PREPARATION: 5 MINS

COOKING TIME: 6 MINS

SERVING PORTIONS: 2

Preparation Process:

1. Preheat the gas grill to medium heat.
2. Spread the butter on the bread slices.
3. Place the sauerkraut and turkey meat directly on the griddle.
4. Place the bread on the other side of the griddle and add 2 slices of cheese to 2 of the slices.
5. Top with the turkey, sauerkraut, and a drizzle of French dressing.
6. Top each bread slice with another slice of bread and cook on the griddle for about 3 mins.
7. Flip over and cook for about 3 mins until both sides are golden.
8. Serve.

Nutrition Values: Cals: 677 Fat: 42g Carbs: 36g Proteins: 37g

Chicken With Mint Chimichurri

Ingredients Needed:

◊ 1 cup of mint leaves
◊ 4 chicken breasts, well cut in half lengthwise
◊ 2/3 cup of parsley leaves
◊ 1 -tbsp full of olive oil
◊ ¼ -tsp of common salt/ sea salt
◊ 1 -tsp full of garlic seasoning
◊ 3 -tbsp full of white vinegar
◊ 2 medium garlic cloves
◊ 2/3 -tsp of red Chili pepper flakes, crushed
◊ 1 -tsp full of Italian Chop House Rub

PREPARATION: 20 MINS

COOKING TIME: 30 MINS

SERVING PORTIONS: 4

Preparation Process:

1. Rub the garlic, red Chili pepper flakes, and Italian Chop House rub on both sides of the chicken.
2. Lightly grease your gas griddle over medium heat. Cook the chicken for about 20 mins.
3. In the meantime, mix the remaining ingredients in a food processor and pulse a few times until well combined.
4. Spread the mixture on top of the cooked chicken and serve.

Nutrition Values: Cals: 335 Fat: 14.7g Carbs: 5.1g Proteins: 43.7g

Chicken Fajitas

Ingredients Needed:

◊ 3 -tbsp full of lime juice
◊ 2 pounds chicken thighs
◊ 2 -tbsp full of olive oil
◊ 2 garlic cloves, grated
◊ 1 and ½ -tsp of cumin
◊ 3 large bell peppers, well cut
◊ 1 onion, well cut
◊ 2 -tbsp full of honey
◊ 1 -tsp full of common salt/sea salt
◊ ½ -tsp of chili powder
◊ 2 well-cut poblano Chili peppers

PREPARATION:
10 MINS

COOKING TIME:
30 MINS

SERVING PORTIONS:
4

Preparation Process:

1. To make the marinade, mix the honey, lime juice, olive oil, garlic cloves, cumin, common salt/ sea salt, and chili powder in a small mixing bowl. Mix thoroughly.
2. Put the chicken thighs in a sealable bag and pour the marinade over them.
3. Close the bag and move the marinade around to make it evenly spread. Allow the chicken to marinate for at least 30 mins (up to 24 hours).
4. Preheat the gas griddle on medium for 10 mins.
5. Spray the griddle with a little oil and put the chicken thighs on it.
6. Cover with a dome and cook for 7 mins, rotating once in between.
7. Remove the chicken thighs after 12 mins of cooking.
8. Squirt a little extra oil on the griddle surface, then add the Chili peppers and onion slices.
9. Toss in the oil, then cover and cook for 5 mins.
10. Toss the vegetables on the griddle and cook them for 5 mins.
11. Seve when ready.

Nutrition Values: Cals: 134 Fat: 71g Carbs: 115g Proteins: 71g

Smoked Turkey Legs

Ingredients Needed:

◊ 4 turkey legs
◊ 2 bay leaves
◊ 1 cup of BBQ rub
◊ 1 ~tbsp full of allspice berries, crushed
◊ 2 ~tsp full of liquid smoke
◊ 4 cups of cold water
◊ 4 cups of ice
◊ 4 cups of warm water
◊ ½ cup of brown sugar
◊ ½ cup of curing common salt/sea salt
◊ 1 ~tbsp full of whole black Chili peppercorns

PREPARATION: 10 MINS

COOKING TIME: 5 HOURS

SERVING PORTIONS: 2

Preparation Process:

1. Place a large stockpot on the stovetop. Add and mix the warm water, curing common salt/sea salt, rub, Chili peppercorns, brown sugar, liquid smoke, allspice, and bay leaves.
2. Bring the mix to a boil on high heat until all the common salt/sea salt granules dissolve thoroughly. Let the mixture cool at room temperature.
3. Add the ice and cold water. Add the turkey legs and ensure they're submerged in the brine. Let the mixture chill in the refrigerator for 24 hours.
4. Drain the turkey legs and discard the brine.
5. Wash off the brine from the legs with the help of cold water, then pat the legs dry.
6. Preheat the gas griddle to low heat.
7. Lay the legs directly on the griddle and close the cover.
8. Smoke the legs for 4–5 hours until their internal temperature reaches 165 °F.
9. Serve and enjoy!

Nutrition Values: Cals: 741 Fat 27.8g Carbs: 39.6g Proteins: 80.1g

Chapter 6
Turkey Recipes

Smoked Young Turkey

Ingredients Needed:

◊ 6/7 medium glasses of olive oil with baked garlic flavor
◊ 1 fresh or defrosted young turkey
◊ Desired seasonings and spices

PREPARATION:
19 – 25 MINS

COOKING TIME:
2 HOURS 10 MINS

SERVING PORTIONS:
6

Preparation Process:

1. Turkey breasts and cavities should be free of extra fat and skin.
2. Slowly peel the turkey skin away from the breast and a portion of the leg leaving the skin intact.
3. Olive oil should be used on the chest, underneath the skin, and on the skin.
4. Rub or season the chest cavity, underneath the skin, and on the skin gently.
5. Preheat your griddle to medium temperature for indirect cooking.
6. Place the turkey meat, chest up, on the griddle.
7. Suck the turkey for around 1 to 2 hours, or till the thickest section of the turkey's chest hits 170°F, and the liquid is clear.
8. Place the turkey in a loose foil tent for around 20 mins before engraving.
9. Serve.

Nutrition Values: Cals: 240 Fat: 9g Carbs: 27g Proteins: 15g

Smokey Whole Turkey

Ingredients Needed:

◊ 2 -tbsp full of well minced fresh parsley
◊ 1 frozen whole turkey, giblets removed, thawed
◊ 1 -tsp full of ground black Chili pepper
◊ 1 cup of butter, unsalted, softened and divided
◊ 2 -tbsp full of orange zest
◊ 1 -tsp full of common salt/ sea salt
◊ ½ cup of water
◊ 2 -tbsp full of well minced fresh rosemary
◊ 14.5-ounces of chicken broth
◊ 2 -tbsp full of well minced fresh sage
◊ 2 -tbsp full of well minced fresh thyme

PREPARATION:
20 MINS

COOKING TIME:
2 HOURS

SERVING PORTIONS:
10

Preparation Process:

1. Preheat your griddle to 180°F till the green light on the dial blinks, indicating that the griddle has attained the desired temperature.
2. In the meantime, prepare the turkey by tucking its wings under it using kitchen twine.
3. In a dish, combine parsley, 1/2 cup of butter, thyme, sage, orange zest, and rosemary; stir well to combine; brush generously on the interior and outside of the turkey; season the external of the turkey with common salt/sea salt and black Chili pepper.
4. Place the turkey breast side up in a roasting pan, pour in the stock and water, add the remaining butter, then place the pan on the griddle.
5. Cook the turkey for 1 hour, then raise the temperature at 350°F and cook for another 1 hour, or till the turkey is well cooked, and the internal temperature reaches 165°F, basting the chicken with the drippings every 30 mins but not in the last hour.
6. Remove the roasting pan out from the griddle and set it aside for around 20 mins to allow the turkey to rest.
7. Carve the turkey into serving pieces.

Nutrition Values: Cals: 146 Fat 8g Carbs: 4g Proteins: 18g

Thanksgiving Turkey

Ingredients Needed:

- ◊ 2 -tsp full of kosher common salt/sea salt
- ◊ 2 cups of butter (softened)
- ◊ 2 -tbsp full of freshly well minced parsley
- ◊ 6 garlic cloves (well minced)
- ◊ 1 -tbsp full of cracked black Chili pepper
- ◊ 2 -tsp full of dried thyme
- ◊ 2 -tbsp full of freshly well minced rosemary
- ◊ 1 (around 18 pounds) turkey
- ◊ 2 -tbsp full of freshly well minced sage

PREPARATION:
20 MINS

COOKING TIME:
3 HOURS

SERVING PORTIONS:
6

Preparation Process:

8. Combine butter, 1 -tsp full of black Chili pepper, thyme, sage, rosemary, parsley, 1 -tsp full of common salt/sea salt, and garlic in a mixing bowl.
1. To loosen the skin out of the turkey, use your fingers.
2. Generously, Rub the butter mixture beneath the skin of the turkey and all over it.
3. Season the turkey liberally with the herb mixture.
4. Preheat your griddle at 300°F for 15 mins with the lid closed.
5. Place your turkey on the griddle and cook for around 3 hours, or till the temperature of the turkey thigh reaches 160°F.
6. Remove the turkey flesh from the griddle and set it aside to cool. Cut into serving sizes and portions.

Per serving: Cals: 278 Fat 31g Carbs: 4g Proteins: 22g

Savory-Sweet Turkey Legs

Ingredients Needed:

◊ ¼ cup of packed light brown sugar
◊ 1 gallon of hot water
◊ 1 -tsp full of ground cloves
◊ 4 turkey legs
◊ 1 cup of curing common salt/ sea salt
◊ 1 -tsp full of freshly ground black Chili pepper
◊ 2 -tsp full of liquid smoke
◊ Mandarin Glaze, for serving
◊ 1 bay leaf

PREPARATION:
10 MINS

COOKING TIME:
3 HOURS

SERVING PORTIONS:
4

Preparation Process:

1. Stir together the water, Chili pepper, curing common salt/sea salt, brown sugar, bay leaf, cloves, and liquid smoke in a large container with a lid till the common salt/ sea salt and sugar are dissolved; set aside to come to room temperature.
2. Refrigerate the turkey legs overnight after submerging them in the seasoned brine.
3. Remove the turkey legs out from the brine and rinse them before cooking; discard the brine.
4. Get your griddle ready. Preheat it to 225°F. Apply a thin layer of oil on the griddle.
5. Place the turkey legs on the griddle, cover, and cook for around 2 to 3 hours, or till dark brown and 165°F on a meat thermometer inserted into the thickest portion of the meat.
6. Serve with a side of Mandarin Glaze or poured on top of the turkey legs.

Nutrition Values: Cals: 190 Fat: 9g Carbs: 5g Proteins: 24g

Brined Turkey Breast

Ingredients Needed:

FOR THE BRINE:

◊ 2 -tbsp full of ground black Chili pepper
◊ 1 cup of brown sugar
◊ 2 pounds of turkey breast, deboned
◊ 4 cups of cold water
◊ ¼ cup of common salt/sea salt

FOR THE BBQ RUB:

◊ 2 -tbsp full of ground black Chili pepper
◊ 2 -tbsp full of red chili powder
◊ 2 -tbsp full of garlic powder
◊ 2 -tbsp full of sugar
◊ 2 -tbsp full of dried onions
◊ 2 -tbsp full of ground cumin
◊ ¼ cup of paprika
◊ 2 -tbsp full of brown sugar
◊ 1 -tbsp full of common salt/sea salt
◊ 1 -tbsp full of cayenne Chili pepper

PREPARATION:
10 MINS

COOKING TIME:
3 HOURS

SERVING PORTIONS:
6

Preparation Process:

1. Prepare the brine by combining black Chili pepper, common salt/ sea salt, and sugar in a large-sized mixing dish, then add water and stir till the sugar has dissolved.
2. Place the turkey breast in it, immerse it well, and refrigerate it for at least 12 hours.
3. Meanwhile, make the BBQ rub by combining all the ingredients in a small-sized mixing bowl and stirring till well blended. Set aside till needed.
4. After that, take the turkey breast out of the brine and season it generously with Prepare BBQ rub.

5. Once you're ready to cook, turn on the griddle, set the temperature at 180°F, and wait at least 15 mins for it to warm.
6. When the griddle has reached temperature, open the lid, set the turkey breast on the griddle grate and cook for around 2 to 3 hours, or till the internal temp reaches 160°F.
7. Transfer the turkey to a cutting board and set it aside for 10 mins before cutting it into slices and serve it

Nutrition Values: Cals: 250 Fat: 5g Carbs: 31g Proteins: 18g

Turkey Legs

Ingredients Needed:

◊ 4 turkey legs

FOR THE BRINE:

◊ ½ cup of brown sugar
◊ 2 ~tsp full of liquid smoke
◊ ½ cup of curing common salt/sea salt
◊ 4 cups of ice
◊ 1 ~tbsp full of whole black Chili peppercorns
◊ 8 cups of cold water
◊ 1 cup of BBQ rub
◊ 2 bay leaves
◊ 16 cups of warm water

PREPARATION:
10 MINS

COOKING TIME:
3 HOURS

SERVING PORTIONS:
4

Preparation Process:

1. To make the brine, fill a large stockpot halfway with heated water, add the Chili peppercorns, bay leaves, and liquid smoke, toss in the common salt/ sea salt, sugar, and BBQ seasoning and bring to the boil.
2. Remove the saucepan from the flame and allow it to cool to room temperature before adding cold water, ice cubes and chilling the brine in the refrigerator.
3. Then put the turkey legs in it, completely submerge them, and refrigerate for 24 hours.
4. Remove the turkey legs out from the brine after 24 hours, rinse thoroughly, and pat dry using paper towels.
5. When you're ready to cook, turn on the griddle, adjust the temperature to 250°F, and wait at least 15 mins for it to warm. Apply a thin layer of oil on the griddle.
6. When the griddle is hot, remove the cover, set the turkey legs on the griddle and cook for around 1 to 2 hours, or till the internal temp hits 165°F.
7. Serve right away.

Nutrition Values: Cals: 216 Fat: 13g Carbs: 5g Proteins: 69g

Herb Roasted Turkey

Ingredients Needed:

◊ 2 ~tbsp full of well minced mixed herbs
◊ ¼ ~tsp full of ground black Chili pepper
◊ 14 pounds of turkey, cleaned
◊ 8 ~tbsp full of butter, unsalted, softened
◊ Pork and poultry rub as needed
◊ 2 cups of chicken broth
◊ 3 ~tbsp full of butter, unsalted and melted

PREPARATION:
15 MINS

COOKING TIME:
2 HOURS
30 MINS

SERVING
PORTIONS:
12

Preparation Process:

1. Remove the giblets from the turkey, wash it inside and out, then wipe it dry using paper towels before placing it on a roasting pan and tucking the turkey wings with butcher's thread.
2. Preheat your griddle for a minimum of 15 mins by turning it on and setting the temperature at 325°F.
3. Meanwhile, make herb butter by placing melted butter in a small-sized mixing bowl, adding black Chili pepper and mixed herbs, and whisking till frothy.
4. Using the handle of a wooden spoon, put some of the Prepare herb butter below the skin of the turkey and massage the skin to properly spread the butter.
5. After that, spread melted butter all over the turkey's exterior, season using pork and poultry rub, and pour the liquid into the roasting pan.
6. When the griddle is hot, remove the cover, lay the roasting pan with the turkey on the griddle and cook for around 2 hours and 30 mins, or till the internal temperature reaches 165°F and the top is golden brown.
7. Transfer the turkey to a chopping board and set aside for 30 mins before carving it into slices and serve it

Nutrition Values:Cals: 155Fat 4gCarbs: 8g Proteins: 29g

Mexican Turkey Patties

Ingredients Needed:

◊ 1 ~tbsp full of taco seasoning
◊ 1 lb. of ground turkey
◊ 1/2 cup of well minced green Chili peppers
◊ Common salt/sea salt to taste

PREPARATION:
15 MINS

COOKING TIME:
10 MINS

SERVING PORTIONS:
4

Preparation Process:

8. In a mixing bowl, combine all the ingredients and stir till well blended.
1. Preheat your griddle to medium-high temperature and apply a thin layer of oil on the griddle.
2. Coat the top of the griddle using cooking spray.
3. Make patties using the ingredients and cook for around 4~5 mins on each side on a hot griddle.
4. Enjoy your meal.

Nutrition Values: Cals: 237 Fat: 13g Carbs: 4g Proteins: 32g

Spinach Turkey Patties

Ingredients Needed:

◊ 5 cups of spinach, sautéed
◊ 3 lbs. of ground turkey
◊ Common salt/sea salt and Chili pepper to taste
◊ 3 ~tbsp full of garlic, well minced
◊ 3 ~tbsp full of mustard
◊ 1 well minced onion

PREPARATION:
10 MINS

COOKING TIME:
10 MINS

SERVING PORTIONS:
12

Preparation Process:

1. In a mixing bowl, combine all of the ingredients and stir till well blended.
2. Preheat your griddle at medium-high. Apply a thin layer of oil on the griddle.
3. Coat the top of the griddle using cooking spray.
4. Make patties using the ingredients and cook for around 5 mins on each side on a hot griddle.
5. Enjoy your meal.

Nutrition Values: Cals: 244 Fat: 13g Proteins: 32g Carbs: 3g

Turkey Sandwich

Ingredients Needed:

◊ 3 oz. of turkey breast, cooked and shredded
◊ 1 cheese slice
◊ 2 bread slices
◊ 1 ~tbsp full of mayonnaise

**PREPARATION:
10 MINS**

**COOKING TIME:
10 MINS**

**SERVING
PORTIONS:
1**

Preparation Process:

1. On one side of each bread slice, spread mayonnaise.
2. Top 1 slice of bread with turkey and cheese
3. Cover with the last slice of bread.
4. Preheat your griddle at medium-high. Apply a thin layer of oil on the griddle.
5. Coat the top of the griddle using cooking spray.
6. Cook the sandwich for around 5 mins on a heated griddle top or till golden brown on both sides.
7. Enjoy your meal.

Nutrition Values: Cals: 307 Fat: 16g Carbs: 16g Proteins: 23g

Chapter 7
Pork Recipes

Flavors Balsamic Pork Chops

Ingredients Needed:

◊ 1/8 ~tsp of chili flakes
◊ 4 pork chops
◊ 2 ~tbsp full of Dijon mustard
◊ 1/2 cup of balsamic vinegar
◊ 1 ~tsp full of dried rosemary
◊ 1/2 ~tsp of Chili pepper
◊ 3/4 ~tsp of common salt/sea salt
◊ 1 ~tsp full of garlic, well minced
◊ 3 ~tbsp full of olive oil

PREPARATION:
10 MINS

COOKING TIME:
15 MINS

SERVING PORTIONS:
4

Preparation Process:

1. In a zip-lock bag combine the pork chops and the additional ingredients. Refrigerate for around 4 hours after sealing the bag and shaking it firmly.
2. Preheat your griddle at medium-high temperature.
3. Coat the top of the griddle using cooking spray.
4. Place the marinated pork chops on a heated griddle top and cook for around 6~8 mins on each side, or till the internal temperature has reached 145°F.
5. Enjoy your meal.

Nutrition Values: Cals: 360 Fat: 31g Carbs: 2g Proteins: 18g

Grilled Pork Chops with Herb Apple Compote

Ingredients Needed:

◊ 1 -tsp full of well minced fresh rosemary
◊ 4, bone-in pork chops
◊ Black Chili pepper
◊ 2 honey-crisp apples, peeled, cored and well minced
◊ Sea common salt/sea salt to taste
◊ 1/3 cup of orange juice
◊ 1 -tsp full of well minced fresh sage

PREPARATION:
10 MINS

COOKING TIME:
20 MINS

SERVING PORTIONS:
4

Preparation Process:

1. In a saucepan, combine the apples, herbs, and orange juice and cook, occasionally stirring till the apples are soft and the juices have thickened to a thin syrup, around 10 to 12 mins.
2. Pork chops should be seasoned using common salt/ sea salt and black Chili pepper.
3. Preheat your griddle to medium-high temperature and apply a thin layer of oil on the griddle.
4. Place the pork chop on the griddle and cook for around 4 mins, till it releases from the griddle.
5. Cook for another 3 mins on the other side.
6. Tent with foil and move to a cutting board.
7. Serve with apple compote on top!

Nutrition Values: Cals: 284 Fat: 20g Carbs: 7g Proteins: 18g

Pork Sausages in White Wine

Ingredients Needed:

◊ 2 glasses of white wine
◊ 8 pork sausages
◊ Olive oil to taste
◊ 2 cloves of garlic

PREPARATION:
10 MINS

COOKING TIME:
50 MINS

SERVING PORTIONS:
4

Preparation Process:

1. Preheat your griddle to 280°F and prepare for indirect cooking.
2. Once the griddle has reached the desired temperature, evenly space the sausages on the griddle.
3. Cook for around 40 mins, turning them over every 5 mins with a little olive oil.
4. Place the wine in a baking dish in the meantime.
5. Garlic should be peeled and washed before being well minced and placed in the baking dish with wine.
6. Remove the sausages from the griddle after 40 mins and heat the wine.
7. Place the sausages in the baking dish once the mixture begins to boil.
8. Allow the sausages to rest for 15 mins after turning off the griddle.
9. Place the sausages on serving dishes after 15 mins.
10. Serve with a sprinkling of wine.

Nutrition Values: Cals: 809 Fat: 32g Carbs: 10g Proteins: 31g

Cuban Pork Chops

Ingredients Needed:

◊ 4 cloves of garlic, smashed
◊ 1/3 cup of lime juice
◊ 1 ~tsp full of ground cumin
◊ 4 pork chops
◊ 2 ~tbsp full of olive oil
◊ 1/4 cup of water
◊ Common salt/sea salt and black Chili pepper to taste

PREPARATION:
20 MINS

COOKING TIME:
1 HOUR
30 MINS

SERVING PORTIONS:
4

Preparation Process:

1. Preheat the griddle at medium temperature. Cook the pork chops till they are lightly browned on both sides after sprinkling common salt/ sea salt on them.
2. In a mixing dish, whisk together the water, garlic, and lime juice till smooth.
3. Continue to cook the pork chops in the lime juice mixture while basting them.
4. Remove the pork chops from the griddle when done cooking and garnish with more sauce and black Chili pepper before serving.

Nutrition Values: Cals: 323 Fat: 27g Carbs: 3g Proteins: 18g

Garlic Soy Pork Chops

Ingredients Needed:

◊ 1/2 cup of olive oil
◊ 4 to 6 pork chops
◊ 1/2 -tsp of common salt/sea salt
◊ 4 cloves of garlic, finely well minced
◊ 1/2 cup of soy sauce
◊ 1/4 cup of butter
◊ 1/2 -tsp of garlic powder
◊ 1/2 -tsp of black Chili pepper

PREPARATION:
20 MINS

COOKING TIME:
1 HOUR

SERVING PORTIONS:
4 TO 6

Preparation Process:

1. Combine the garlic, soy sauce, olive oil, and garlic powder in a big zip-lock bag. Place the pork chops in the marinade and ensure they are well coated. Allow 30 mins for preparation.
2. Preheat your griddle at medium-high. Add two -tbsp full of oil and two -tbsp full of butter to the griddle.
3. Place the chops on the griddle one at a time, being careful not to crowd them. Cook the chops for around 5 mins on the griddle with an additional 2 -tbsp full of butter. Cook for another 4 mins.
4. Remove the chops out from the griddle and brush them with the remaining butter.
5. Serve after 5 mins of resting.

Nutrition Values: Cals: 398 Fat: 38g Carbs: 4g Proteins: 14g

Paprika Dijon Pork Tenderloin

Ingredients Needed:

◊ 2 ~tbsp full of Dijon mustard
◊ 1 ~tsp full of common salt/sea salt
◊ 2 1 lb. pork tenderloins
◊ 2 ~tbsp full of olive oil
◊ 1 and 1/2 ~tsp of smoked paprika

PREPARATION:
10 MINS

COOKING TIME:
4 HOURS

SERVING PORTIONS:
6

Preparation Process:

1. Combine the mustard and paprika in a small-sized mixing bowl.
2. Preheat your griddle at medium. Apply a thin layer of oil on the griddle.
3. Make sure the tenderloins are evenly coated with the mustard mixture.
4. Cook the tenderloins on the griddle till nicely browned on all sides and the internal temperature reaches 135°F.
5. Before slicing and serving remove the tenderloins out from the griddle and let them rest for 5 mins.

Nutrition Values: Cals: 484 Fat: 25g Carbs: 14g Proteins: 51g

Pineapple Honey Pork Chops

Ingredients Needed:

◊ 1 -tbsp full of Dijon mustard
◊ 1 cup of crushed pineapple
◊ 4 pork chops, boneless
◊ Common salt/sea salt and Chili pepper to taste
◊ 1/4 cup of honey

PREPARATION:
10 MINS

COOKING TIME:
15 MINS

SERVING PORTIONS:
4

Preparation Process:

1. In a zip-lock bag combine the pork chops and the additional ingredients. Refrigerate overnight after sealing the bag and shaking it well.
2. Preheat your griddle at medium-high.
3. Coat the top of the griddle using cooking spray.
4. Cook pork chops for around 5-6 mins on each side on a heated griddle top.
5. Enjoy your meal.

Nutrition Values: Cals: 351 Fat: 20g Carbs: 25g Proteins: 19g

Pork Patties

Ingredients Needed:

◊ 1/2 -tsp of onion powder
◊ 1 lb. of ground pork
◊ 1/2 -tsp of dried thyme
◊ 3/4 -tsp of fennel seeds
◊ 1/8 -tsp of red Chili pepper, crushed
◊ 1 -tsp full of garlic powder
◊ 3/4 -tsp of Chili pepper
◊ 1/2 -tsp of common salt/sea salt
◊ 1/8 -tsp of ground nutmeg
◊ 3/4 -tsp of ground sage

PREPARATION:
10 MINS

COOKING TIME:
15 MINS

SERVING PORTIONS:
4

Preparation Process:

1. In a mixing bowl, combine all the ingredients and stir till well blended.
2. Preheat your griddle at medium-high.
3. Coat the top of the griddle using cooking spray.
4. Make patties using the ingredients and cook for around 5 mins on each side on a hot griddle.
5. Enjoy your meal.

Nutrition Values: Cals: 85 Fat: 2g Carbs: 2g Proteins: 15g

Citrusy Butter Pork Chops

Ingredients Needed:

◊ 2 lemons, well cut into wedges
◊ 1 clove of garlic, well minced
◊ 1 -tsp full of black Chili pepper
◊ 2 oranges, well cut into wedges
◊ 6 sprigs of rosemary, well minced
◊ 5 pork chops
◊ 2 sticks of butter, softened
◊ 4 -tbsp full of fresh thyme leave, well minced

PREPARATION:
10 MINS

COOKING TIME:
30 MINS

SERVING PORTIONS:
4

Preparation Process:

1. Preheat your griddle at medium temperature and apply a thin layer of oil on the griddle.
2. In a dish, squeeze the lemons and oranges. Except for the pork chops, combine the remaining ingredients in a mixing bowl.
3. Marinate the pork chops for around 3 hours in the mixture. Cook for around 10 mins per side on the griddle.
4. Serve when ready.

Nutrition Values: Cals: 396 Fat: 17g Carbs: 7g Proteins: 32g

Soy Honey Pork Chops

Ingredients Needed:

◊ 1/4 cup of organic honey
◊ 2 -tbsp full of olive oil
◊ 6 (4 ounces) of boneless pork chops
◊ 1 to 2 -tbsp full of low-sodium soy sauce
◊ 1 -tbsp full of rice mirin

PREPARATION:
20 MINS

COOKING TIME:
25 MINS

SERVING PORTIONS:
6

Preparation Process:

1. Whisk together the honey, oil, soy sauce, and white vinegar till completely blended. In a big sealable plastic bag combine the sauce and pork chops and marinate for 1 hour.
2. Preheat your griddle at medium-high and cook the pork chop for around 4 to 5 mins, or till it easily slides off the griddle.
3. Cook for around 5 mins more on the other side, or till the internal temperature has reached 145°F.
4. Enjoy your meal!

Nutrition Values: Cals: 251 Fat: 9g Carbs: 13g Proteins: 30g

Marinated Pork Chops

Ingredients Needed:

◊ 1 -tsp full of garlic, well minced
◊ 4 pork chops
◊ 1/3 cup of Worcestershire sauce
◊ 1/4 -tsp of cayenne
◊ 2 -tbsp full of olive oil
◊ 1/2 -tsp of Chili pepper
◊ Common salt/sea salt to taste
◊ 1/4 cup of soy sauce
◊ 1/3 cup of balsamic vinegar

PREPARATION:
10 MINS

COOKING TIME:
10 MINS

SERVING PORTIONS:
4

Preparation Process:

1. In a zip-lock bag combine the pork chops and the additional ingredients. Refrigerate for around 4 hours after sealing the bag and shaking it firmly.
2. Preheat your griddle at medium-high temperature.
3. Coat the top of the griddle using cooking spray.
4. Place the marinated pork chops onto a hot griddle top and cook for around 3-5 mins on each side, or till the internal temperature reaches 145°F.
5. Enjoy your meal.

Nutrition Values: Cals: 351 Fat: 27g Carbs: 6g Proteins: 19g

Simple and Easy Grilled Pork Tenderloin

Ingredients Needed:

◊ 1 batch of Pork Rub
◊ 2 (around 1-pound/454 g) pork tenderloins

PREPARATION:
10 MINS

COOKING TIME:
4 HOURS

SERVING PORTIONS:
6

Preparation Process:

1. Preheat your griddle to 250°F and apply a thin layer of oil on the griddle.
2. Season the tenderloins well using the rub. Work the rub into the meat using your hands.
3. Put the tenderloins directly on the griddle and cook for around 4 to 5 hours, or till they reach 145°F (63°C) internal temperature.
4. Remove the tenderloins out from the griddle and set them to rest for 5–10 mins before slicing thinly and serving.

Nutrition Values: Cals: 364 Fat: 22g Proteins: 37g Carbs: 3g

Chapter 8
Beef Recipes

High-Low Strip Steak

Ingredients Needed:

◊ 2 (1-pound / 454-g) New York strip steaks, trimmed

FOR THE RUB:

◊ 1 bunch of thyme sprigs
◊ 1 bunch of rosemary sprigs
◊ 1 bunch of sage sprigs
◊ 1 and ½ -tsp of black Chili pepper, divided
◊ ¾ -tsp of sea common salt/sea salt, divided
◊ ½ -tsp of garlic powder
◊ 2 -tbsp full of well minced fresh flat-leaf parsley
◊ 2 -tbsp full of extra-virgin olive oil

PREPARATION:
10 MINS

COOKING TIME:
15 MINS

SERVING PORTIONS:
2

Preparation Process:

1. Preheat the griddle to high heat. Combine rub fixings in a small mixing bowl and rub steaks with spice mixture; let rest for 10 mins.
2. Place steaks on the griddle and cook for 1 minute per side. Turn the griddle down to medium heat.
3. Turn steaks and grill for 3 additional mins per side; or until the thermometer registers 135°F (57°C) for medium rare.
4. Remove steaks to a platter. Let rest for 5 mins. Cut steaks across the grain into thin slices.
5. Serve.

Nutrition Values: Cals: 400 Fat: 20g Carbs: 0g Proteins: 40g

Caprese Flank Steak

Ingredients Needed:

◊ 4 (6-ounce / 170-g) flank steaks
◊ Sea common salt/sea salt, for seasoning
◊ Flakey common salt/sea salt, for serving
◊ Fresh ground Chili pepper, to taste
◊ Olive oil to taste
◊ 2 Roma tomatoes, well cut
◊ 4 ounces (113 g) of fresh buffalo mozzarella, cut into four slices
◊ 8 fresh basil leaves
◊ Balsamic vinegar glaze, for drizzling

PREPARATION:
10 MINS

COOKING TIME:
10 MINS

SERVING PORTIONS:
4

Preparation Process:

1. Lightly brush each filet, on all sides, with olive oil and season with common salt/ sea salt and Chili pepper. Preheat the griddle to high. Place steaks on the griddle, reduce heat to medium, tent with foil and cook for 5 mins.
2. Flip, re-tent, and cook for an additional 5 mins; during the last 2 mins of cooking top each with a slice of mozzarella.
3. Remove steaks from the griddle and top each with a few tomato slices and 2 basil leaves. Drizzle with balsamic glaze, and sprinkle with flakey common salt/sea salt and a little blacker Chili pepper.
4. Serve

Nutrition Values:Cals: 368 Fat: 23g Carbs: 14g Proteins: 22g

Steak with Cheese

Ingredients Needed:

◊ 1 (24-ounce / 680-g) dry-aged New York strip steak
◊ Common salt/sea salt and Chili pepper, for coating
◊ ½ cup blue cheese
◊ 2 -tbsp full of oil

PREPARATION:
6 MINS

COOKING TIME:
8 MINS

SERVING PORTIONS:
4

Preparation Process:

1. Preheat the griddle to medium-high heat. Pat your steak dry and coat it with common salt/ sea salt and Chili pepper. Let sit for 20 to 30 mins. Place the steak over high heat for 5 mins, then flip and repeat.
2. Move to medium heat and cook for another 2 to 3 mins. Move it to a cutting board and let rest for 10 mins.
3. While the steak is cooling combine the cheese and oil in a food processor and blend until smooth and fluffy, about 1 minute.
4. Slice the steak then top with the blue cheese mixture just before serving.

Nutrition Values: Cals: 330 Fat: 16g Carbs: 31g Proteins: 15g

Caprese Grilled Filet Mignon

Ingredients Needed:

◊ 4 (6-ounce / 170-g) filets
◊ 1 -tsp full of garlic common salt/sea salt
◊ Olive oil to taste
◊ 2 Roma tomatoes, well cut
◊ 4 ounces fresh buffalo mozzarella, cut into four slices
◊ 8 fresh basil leaves
◊ Balsamic vinegar glaze, for drizzling
◊ Sea common salt/sea salt, for seasoning
◊ Fresh ground Chili pepper to taste

PREPARATION:
10 MINS

COOKING TIME:
10 MINS

SERVING PORTIONS:
4

Preparation Process:

1. Lightly brush each filet, on all sides, with olive oil and rub with garlic common salt/sea salt. Preheat the griddle to high. Place steaks on the griddle, reduce heat to medium, tent with foil and cook for 5 mins.
2. Flip, re-tent, and cook for an additional 5 mins; during the last 2 mins of grilling top each with a slice of Mozzarella.
3. Remove steaks from the griddle and top each with a few tomato slices and 2 basil leaves. Drizzle with balsamic, sprinkle with sea common salt/ sea salt and black Chili pepper and serve.

Nutrition Values: Cals: 227 Fat: 15g Carbs: 0g Proteins: 22g

Flank Steak with Garlic and Rosemary

Ingredients Needed:

◊ 2 (8-ounce / 227-g) flank steaks

FOR THE MARINADE:

◊ 1 -tbsp full of extra-virgin olive oil, plus more for brushing
◊ 2 -tbsp full of fresh rosemary, well minced
◊ 4 cloves garlic, well minced
◊ 2 -tsp full of sea common salt/sea salt
◊ ¼ -tsp of black Chili pepper

PREPARATION:
10 MINS

COOKING TIME:
20 MINS

SERVING PORTIONS:
4

Preparation Process:

1. Add marinade fixings to a food processor or blender and pulse until garlic and rosemary are pulverized. Use a fork to pierce the steaks 10 times on each side.
2. Rub each evenly with the marinade on both sides. Put in a covered dish and refrigerate for at least 1 hour or overnight.
3. Preheat the griddle to high and brush with olive oil and preheat to high. Cook steaks for 5 mins, flip, tent with foil, and cook for about 3-4 mins more.
4. Transfer meat to rest on a cutting board and cover with aluminum foil, for about 15 mins.
5. Slice and serve immediately.

Nutrition Values: Cals: 449 Fat: 28g Carbs: 5g Proteins: 44g

Rib Eye Steak with Butter

Ingredients Needed:

◊ 1 unpeeled white or red onion
◊ Oil for coating
◊ 1 ~tbsp full of molasses (may substitute honey)
◊ 1 ~tbsp full of butter
◊ Common salt/sea salt, for seasoning and coating
◊ 1 (1~pound / 454~g) bone-in rib eye steak, about 1½ inches thick
◊ Chili Pepper for coating

PREPARATION:
10 MINS

COOKING TIME:
30 MINS

SERVING PORTIONS:
1

Preparation Process:

1. Preheat the griddle to medium-high heat and brush with oil. Roast the onion directly onto the griddle until it feels soft when prodded with tongs, about 20 mins.
2. Move it to a cutting board, remove the skin, and chop the flesh finely. Add the onion and cook until it's deep brown.
3. Add the molasses and cook for another 5 mins, then add the butter, season with common salt/ sea salt, and keep the sauce warm on a corner of the grill while you cook the rib eye.
4. Coat the steak generously with common salt/ sea salt and Chili pepper and let sit for 20 to 30 mins. Preheat griddle to high heat and sear for about 6 mins per side, turning often, until it's deeply browned.
5. Remove from heat when an instant-read meat thermometer, placed in the thickest part, reads 130°F (54°C).
6. Transfer to a serving plate and let sit for 10 mins before serving with the caramelized onions.

Nutrition Values:Cals: 165 Fat: 9g Carbs: 0g Proteins: 21g

Chapter 9

Fish And Seafood Recipes

Lemon Garlic Shrimp

Ingredients Needed:

◊ 1 and ½ lb. of shrimp, peeled and deveined
◊ 1 -tbsp full of garlic, well minced
◊ ¼ cup of butter
◊ ¼ cup of fresh parsley, well minced
◊ ¼ cup of fresh lemon juice
◊ Common salt/sea salt and Chili peppers to taste

Preparation Process:

1. Preheat the griddle to high heat.
2. Melt butter on the griddle top.
3. Add garlic and sauté for 30 seconds.
4. Add shrimp and season with Chili pepper and common salt/ sea salt and cook for 4–5 mins or until it turns pink.
5. Add lemon juice and parsley and stir well and cook for 2 mins.
6. Serve when ready!

Nutrition Values: Cals: 312 Carbs: 3.9g Fat: 14.6g Proteins: 39.2g

PREPARATION: 15 – 20 MINS

COOKING TIME: 15 MINS

SERVING PORTIONS: 4

Spicy Lemon Butter Shrimp

Ingredients Needed:

◊ 1 and ½ lb. of shrimp, peeled and deveined
◊ 3 garlic cloves, well minced
◊ 1 small onion, well minced
◊ ½ cup of butter
◊ 1 and ½ ~tbsp of fresh parsley, well minced
◊ 1 ~tbsp full of fresh lemon juice
◊ ¼ ~tsp of red Chili pepper flakes
◊ Common salt/sea salt and Chili peppers to taste

PREPARATION:
15 – 20 MINS

COOKING TIME:
10 MINS

SERVING PORTIONS:
4

Preparation Process:

1. Preheat the griddle to high heat.
2. Melt butter on the griddle top.
3. Add garlic, onion, red chili flakes, Chili pepper, and common salt/ sea salt and stir for 2 mins.
4. Season shrimp with Chili pepper and common salt/ sea salt and thread onto skewers.
5. Brush shrimp skewers with butter mixture.
6. Place shrimp skewers on griddle top and cook until shrimp turns pink, about 3–4 mins.
7. Transfer the shrimp to the serving plate.
8. Drizzle lemon juice over shrimp and garnish with parsley.
9. Serve when ready!

Nutrition Values: Cals: 419 Fat: 25g Carbs: 5.2g Proteins: 39.4g

Italian Shrimp

Ingredients Needed:

◊ 1 lb. of shrimp, deveined
◊ 1 -tsp full of Italian seasoning
◊ 1 -tsp full of paprika
◊ 1 and ½ -tsp of garlic, well minced
◊ 1 stick of butter
◊ 1 fresh lemon juice
◊ ¼ -tsp of Chili pepper
◊ ½ -tsp of common salt/sea salt

PREPARATION:
15 – 20 MINS

COOKING TIME:
5 MINS

SERVING PORTIONS:
4

Preparation Process:

1. Preheat the griddle to high heat.
2. Melt butter on the hot griddle top.
3. Add garlic and cook for 30 seconds.
4. Toss shrimp with paprika, Italian seasoning Chili pepper, and common salt/ sea salt.
5. Add shrimp into the pan and cook for 2–3 mins per side.
6. Drizzle lemon juice over the shrimp.
7. Stir and serve when ready!

Nutrition Values: Cals: 346 Fat: 25g Carbs: 2.6g Proteins: 26.2g

Salmon Lime Burgers

Ingredients Needed:

◊ 2 hamburger buns, well cut in half
◊ 1 ~tbsp full of cilantro, fresh well minced
◊ 1/8 ~tsp of fresh ground Chili pepper
◊ ½ lb. of salmon fillets, skinless, cubed
◊ ½ ~tbsp of grated lime zest
◊ ¼ ~tsp of sea common salt/sea salt, fine ground
◊ 1 and ½ garlic cloves, well minced
◊ ½ ~tbsp of Dijon mustard
◊ 1 and ½ ~tbsp of shallots, finely well minced
◊ ½ ~tbsp of honey
◊ ½ ~tbsp of soy sauce

PREPARATION:
15 – 20 MINS

COOKING TIME:
10 MINS

SERVING PORTIONS:
2

Preparation Process:

1. Mix all of your ingredients in a mixing bowl, except the hamburger buns.
2. Make 2 burger patties that are ½-inch thick with this mixture.
3. Preheat your griddle grill to a medium-temperature setting.
4. Once your grill is preheated, place the 2 patties on the grill.
5. Grill your patties for 5 mins per side.
6. Serve on warm buns and enjoy!

Nutrition Values: Cals: 220 Fat: 15g Carbs: 6g Proteins: 16g

Caper Basil Halibut

Ingredients Needed:

◊ 24 oz. of halibut fillets
◊ 2 garlic cloves, crushed
◊ 2 ~tbsp full of olive oil
◊ 2 ~tsp full of capers, drained
◊ 3 ~tbsp full of fresh basil, well cut
◊ 2 and ½ ~tbsp of fresh lemon juice

PREPARATION:
15 – 20 MINS

COOKING TIME:
8 MINS

SERVING PORTIONS:
4

Preparation Process:

1. In a small mixing bowl, whisk together garlic, olive oil, and lemon juice. Stir in 2 ~tbsp full of basil.
2. Season garlic mixture with Chili pepper and common salt/ sea salt.
3. Season fish fillets with Chili pepper and common salt/ sea salt and brush with garlic mixture.
4. Preheat the griddle to high heat.
5. Place fish fillets on a hot griddle and cook for 4 mins on each side.
6. Transfer the fish fillets to serving plate and top with the remaining garlic mixture and basil.
7. Serve when ready!

Nutrition Values: Cals: 250 Fat: 10.5g Carbs: 0.8g Proteins: 39.1g

Grilled Prawns with Roasted Garlic and Dill Butter

Ingredients Needed:

◊ 6 to 8 giant prawns
◊ 2 ~tbsp full of olive oil
◊ 1 ~tsp full of sea common salt/sea salt
◊ 2 lemons, cut in half
◊ Roasted garlic and dill butter

PREPARATION:
15 – 20 MINS

COOKING TIME:
3 MINS

SERVING PORTIONS:
4

Preparation Process:

1. Using a sharp knife, slice prawns in half lengthwise from head to tail. Pull meat from the shell, leaving the tail attached, and remove the vein.
2. Rinse the prawn halves under cold water to remove the organs and internals from the head area.
3. Tuck meat back into the shell and drizzle prawn halves with olive oil and sea common salt/ sea salt.
4. Bring the griddle grill to high heat. Oil the griddle and allow it to heat. Place lemon halves, cut side down, over direct heat, and grill till evenly charred.
5. Place prawns over direct heat, meat side down, and grill for 2 to 3 mins depending on the size of the prawns.
6. Flip prawns to meat side up and top with garlic and dill butter. Cook an additional 3 mins, allowing the butter to melt on and around the meat inside the shell.
7. Remove from the grill and serve with charred lemon.

Nutrition Values: Cals: 248 Fat: 2.7g Carbs: 31.4g Proteins: 24.9g

Scallops

Ingredients Needed:

◊ Large Fresh Bay Scallops
◊ Real Butter, Melted
◊ Common salt/sea salt and Chili pepper to Taste

PREPARATION:
15 – 20 MINS

COOKING TIME:
10 MINS

SERVING PORTIONS:
4

Preparation Process:

1. Preheat the griddle grill to high.
2. Melt the butter and set it aside so that it is ready for later.
3. Season the scallops with common salt/ sea salt and Chili pepper.
4. Spray the grill with spray oil, and immediately place the scallops on the heat. Brush the tops with butter.
5. Grill for 3–4 mins per side, brushing with the butter again after flipping. The scallops are ready to turn when they pull away easily from the grill.
6. Brush the scallops again with the butter, and grill for an additional thirty seconds per side.
7. Let the scallops relax for 5 mins before serving.

Nutrition Values: Cals: 1070 Fat: 89g Carbs: 240g Proteins: 77g

Hibachi Salmon

Ingredients Needed:

◊ 2 lbs. of salmon fillets
◊ ½ cup of teriyaki sauce
◊ 1 -tsp full of freshly grated ginger
◊ 2 cloves garlic
◊ ¼ cup of brown sugar
◊ 2 -tsp full of black Chili pepper
◊ 1 -tbsp full of maple syrup

PREPARATION:
15 – 20 MINS

COOKING TIME:
10 MINS

SERVING PORTIONS:
4

Preparation Process:

1. Mix all the ingredients together in a covered glass mixing bowl or resealable bag and refrigerate for several hours overnight.
2. Heat the griddle grill to high and grill the salmon fillets for 3–4 mins per side until cooked through. Salmon should be homogeneous in color with white juice between the flakes.
3. Let rest for several mins before serving.

Nutrition Values: Cals: 251 Fat: 13g Carbs: 3g Proteins: 30g

Summer Shrimp Salad

Ingredients Needed:

◊ ½ pint of cherry tomatoes
◊ 3 -tbsp full of olive oil
◊ ½ -tsp of common salt/sea salt
◊ 1 pound medium to thin asparagus, woody stems snapped off and discarded
◊ 1 pound shelled and deveined medium shrimp
◊ ¼ -tsp of freshly ground black Chili pepper
◊ ¼ -tsp of dried thyme
◊ Grated zest and juice of ½ lemon

PREPARATION:
15 – 20 MINS

COOKING TIME:
3 MINS

SERVING PORTIONS:
5

Preparation Process:

1. Quarter the cherry tomatoes and put them in a medium mixing bowl. Add 1 -tbsp full of olive oil and ¼ -tsp of common salt/sea salt. Toss gently and set aside.

2. In a medium mixing bowl, pour 1 -tbsp full of olive oil over the asparagus spears and rub gently to coat them.

3. Turn the control knob to the high position. Oil the griddle and allow it to heat until the oil is shimmering but not smoking. Grill the asparagus for about 5 mins. The thicker ones will still have a bit of crunch to them and the thinner ones will be tender. Transfer to a cutting board; keep the griddle on high. When they are cool enough to handle, cut the spears into 1-inch pieces. Add to the cherry tomatoes.

4. Rinse the shrimp and pat dry with paper towels. Put them in a medium mixing bowl, add the remaining -tbsp full of olive oil, and toss to coat. Grill the shrimp for about 3 mins, until they are opaque and firm to the touch.

5. Add the shrimp to the tomatoes and asparagus. Add the remaining ¼ -tsp full of common salt/sea salt, Chili pepper, thyme, and lemon juice, and zest, and toss to combine.

6. Serve warm or at room temperature or refrigerate and serve chilled.

Nutrition Values: Cals: 240 Fat: 13g Proteins: 25g

Chapter 10
Game Recipes

Brisket Sandwich

Ingredients Needed:

◊ 1 well cut white onion
◊ 2 -tbsp full of butter
◊ 2 -tbsp full of olive oil
◊ 15 slices of leftover brisket
◊ Common salt/sea salt and Chili pepper to taste
◊ 2 jalapenos, thinly well cut
◊ 4 brioche buns
◊ 8 extra sharp cheddar cheese, well cut

PREPARATION:
15 MINS

COOKING TIME:
15 MINS

SERVING PORTIONS:
4

Preparation Process:

1. Preheat your gas griddle to 350°F.
2. Preheat a cast-iron pan on the griddle. Combine the olive oil and butter. Add onions, common salt/sea salt, and Chili pepper after the butter has melted. Cook onions till golden brown and soft.
3. Mix the jalapenos with the onions. Allow 3-4 mins for the jalapenos to fry. Place the cheese slices on top and allow them to melt.
4. Cook the buns to make them toasty on the griddle. When the buns are toasted, top them with well-cut brisket, onion, jalapenos, and cheese.
5. Serve with a dipping sauce of your choice.

Nutrition Values: Cals: 452 Fat: 32g Carbs: 22g Proteins: 18g

Mac and Cheese Quesadilla

Ingredients

◊ 2 cups heavy cream
◊ 2 cups cheddar, shredded
◊ 1 ~tbsp full of cornstarch
◊ 2 ~tbsp full of butter
◊ 2 cups elbow macaroni, cooked
◊ 4 (8~in.) tortillas
◊ 12 slices American cheese, yellow
◊ 1/2 ~tsp of sea common salt/sea salt
◊ 1/2 ~tsp of ground black Chili pepper

PREPARATION:
10 MINS

COOKING TIME:
20 MINS

SERVING PORTIONS:
4

Preparation Process:

1. Heavy cream should be brought to a boil in a separate container.
2. In a mixing bowl, combine the cheddar cheese and cornstarch.
3. When the cream is boiling stir in the butter and cheddar cheese combination.
4. Stir in macaroni until well incorporated. Set aside to cool.
5. Arrange 1 tortilla on the griddle grill pan. Top with 3 slices of American cheese, 1 cup of mac and cheese, and 3 more slices of American cheese. Add little common salt/ sea salt and Chili pepper before serving. Add a second tortilla to complete the dish.
6. Grill the quesadilla until the cheese is melted and the tortilla is cooked. Repeat to make the second quesadilla.
7. Serve and enjoy

Nutrition Values: Cals: 1020 Fat: 49g Carbs: 111g Proteins: 34g

Buffalo Chicken Dip

Ingredients Needed:

◊ 2 cups of cooked chicken, shredded
◊ ½ cup of RedHot Sauce
◊ Chips, crostini, crackers, or well-cut vegetables for serving
◊ ½ cup of sour cream
◊ 1 -tsp full of kosher common salt/sea salt
◊ ½ cup of blue cheese
◊ 1 cup of cream cheese, softened
◊ ½ cup of mayonnaise
◊ 4 strips of cooked bacon, crumbled
◊ ½ cup of mayonnaise
◊ 1 cup of shredded mozzarella cheese
◊ 1 cup of shredded cheddar cheese
◊ 2 -tbsp full of dry ranch seasoning

PREPARATION:
10 MINS

COOKING TIME:
30 MINS

SERVING PORTIONS:
6

Preparation Process:

1. Preheat your gas griddle to 350°F.
2. Combine cream cheese, common salt/ sea salt, sour cream, mayonnaise, ranch dressing and spicy sauce in a medium-sized mixing dish or the mixing bowl of the stand mixer.
3. Combine the cheddar, mozzarella, and shredded chicken. Move to an ovenproof dish and cover with crumbled bacon and blue cheese.
4. Cook for around 20 to 30 mins, till the top, is golden brown and the dip is bubbling directly on the griddle.
5. Serve with crostini, chips, crackers, or veggies well cut thinly. Enjoy!

Nutrition Values: Cals: 246 Fat: 21g Carbs: 2g Proteins: 11g

Bloomin Onion Bites

Ingredients Needed:

FOR ONION BITES:

◊ 1 ~tbsp full of Chili pepper
◊ 2 bags of pearl onions
◊ 1 pint of buttermilk
◊ 2 cups of all~purpose flour
◊ 1 ~tsp full of cayenne Chili pepper
◊ 1 ~tbsp full of paprika
◊ Vegetable oil for frying
◊ 1 ~tbsp full of kosher common salt/sea salt
◊ 2 eggs

FOR THE DIP:

◊ 1 ~tbsp full of ketchup
◊ ¼ cup of sour cream
◊ ¼ cup of mayonnaise
◊ Common salt/sea salt and Chili pepper to taste
◊ ½ ~tsp of paprika

**PREPARATION:
15 MINS**

**COOKING TIME:
25 MINS**

**SERVING
PORTIONS:
6**

Preparation Process:

1. Preheat your gas griddle to 350°F.
2. Combine the eggs and buttermilk in a mixing bowl. To make four portions, peel the onions, cut off their roots, and make two slices 3/4 down from the root to the tip. Allow 30 mins for the onions to soak in the buttermilk egg mixture.
3. Heat the oil in the fry pot on the griddle.
4. Combine flour, common salt/sea salt, paprika, Chili pepper and cayenne Chili pepper. Roll the onions in the flour mixture, making sure to get flour between the layers and portions. Fry onions till golden brown.
5. Serve.

Nutrition Values: Cals: 47 Fat: 2g Carbs: 6g Proteins: 2g

Chimichurri Sauce

Ingredients Needed:

◊ ¼ cup of extra-virgin olive oil
◊ 1 -tsp full of common salt/sea salt
◊ 4 cloves garlic, well diced
◊ 2 whole lemons, halved
◊ 2 medium flat-leaf Italian parsley, washed and well minced
◊ ½ -tsp of black Chili pepper
◊ ¼ cup of red wine vinegar

PREPARATION:
10 MINS

COOKING TIME:
5 MINS

SERVING PORTIONS:
4

Preparation Process:

1. Preheat your gas griddle to 450°F and apply a thin layer of oil on top of the griddle.
2. Cook for around 5 mins, or till charred, by placing the lemon halves on the griddle.
3. Remove the lemons from the griddle and squeeze them. In a food processor, combine all ingredients and puree till smooth, or leave somewhat lumpy for texture.
4. If you like a milder flavor, add more olive oil to taste.
5. Serve as a side dish or a dip.

Nutrition Values: Cals: 145 Fat: 14g Carbs: 6g Proteins: 1g

Honey Sriracha Chex Mix

Ingredients Needed:

◊ 1 cup of pretzels
◊ ¼ cup of honey
◊ 2 cups roasted peanuts
◊ ¼ cup of sriracha sauce
◊ 6 cups corn Chex
◊ 4 -tbsp full of butter
◊ 1 cup of bag popcorn
◊ 6 cups of rice Chex

PREPARATION:
105MINS

COOKING TIME:
1 HOUR

SERVING
PORTIONS:
4

Preparation Process:

1. Preheat your gas griddle to 350°F. Combine all dry ingredients in a large-sized mixing dish.
2. Melt butter in a large-sized roasting pan or Dutch oven on the griddle, then add Sriracha and honey.
3. Gradually drizzle in the cereal mixture till it is evenly coated.
4. Cook for around 1 hour, tossing every 15 mins. To cool, spread on parchment paper.
5. Keep it in an airtight container until it's time to serve.

Nutrition Values: Cals: 314 Fat: 35g Carbs: 42g Proteins: 26g

Mandarin Wings

Ingredients Needed:

◊ Pounds of chicken wings, flats, and drumettes separated
◊ Chicken rub, as needed
◊ 12 ounces of mandarin orange sauce

PREPARATION:
10 MINS

COOKING TIME:
30 MINS

SERVING PORTIONS:
2

Preparation Process:

1. Using mandarin sauce, coat the chicken wings. Rub the wings using Beef Rub and Chicken Rub. Allow for 30 mins of marination.
2. Preheat your gas griddle to 350°F and apply a thin layer of oil on top of the griddle.
3. Cook the wings for around 30 mins on the griddle.
4. Enjoy!

Nutrition Values: Cals: 207 Fat: 7g Carbs: 9.79g Proteins: 28g

Ultimate Game Day Dip

Ingredients Needed:

◊ 1 cup of shredded cheddar cheese
◊ ½ cup of shredded Parmesan cheese
◊ 1 cup of mayonnaise
◊ ½ cup of well minced scallions
◊ Chips, crostini, or vegetables for serving
◊ 6 jalapeños, seeded, ribs removed and finely well diced
◊ 1 pound cream cheese, softened
◊ 8 slices of bacon, cooked and well minced

FOR THE TOPPING:

◊ 1 cup of panko breadcrumbs
◊ ½ cup of shredded Parmesan cheese
◊ ¼ cup of butter, melted

PREPARATION:
10 MINS

COOKING TIME:
30 MINS

SERVING PORTIONS:
6

Preparation Process:

1. Preheat your gas griddle to 350°F.
2. Combine cream cheese and mayonnaise in the dish of a stand mixer and beat with a paddle attachment till smooth. Combine the remaining ingredients for the dip in a mixing bowl.
3. Smooth the top of the dip in a cast-iron skillet. To make the topping combine all of the ingredients and put it on top of your dip. Cook for around 20 to 30 mins on the griddle until the top is gently browned and the dip is bubbling on the griddle.
4. Serve with crostini, dipping chips, or vegetables. Enjoy!

Nutrition Values: Cals: 78Kcal Fat: 4g Carbs: 2g Proteins: 7g

Asian Spiced Cornish Hen

Ingredients

◊ 1 cornish hen
◊ 1 and ½ -tsp of Chinese five-spice powder
◊ 1 and ½ -tsp of rice wine
◊ ½ -tsp of Chili pepper
◊ 2 cups of water
◊ 3 -tbsp full of soy sauce
◊ 2 -tbsp full of sugar
◊ Common salt/sea salt to taste

PREPARATION:
10 MINS

COOKING TIME:
60 MINS

SERVING PORTIONS:
2

Preparation Process:

1. Put the water, soy sauce, rice wine, five-spice, Chili pepper and common salt/sea salt in a large mixing bowl and whisk together until smooth.
2. Refrigerate overnight with the Cornish hen in the basin.
3. Preheat the griddle to high heat. Use frying spray to coat the griddle's top.
4. Remove the Cornish hen from the marinade and cook on a hot griddle top for sixty mins, or until the internal temp reaches 185°F, depending on the size of the hen.
5. Serve with a knife and fork.

Nutrition Values: Cals: 233 Fat: 11.8g Carbs: 15.9g Proteins: 15.9g

Chapter 11

Appetizers, Snacks And Desserts

Potato Fries

Ingredients Needed:

◊ 2 pounds peeled and cut into ½-inch wedges of sweet potatoes
◊ 2 -tbsp full of olive oil
◊ Chili pepper and common salt/sea salt to taste

PREPARATION:
5 MINS

COOKING TIME:
12 MINS

SERVING PORTIONS:
2

Preparation Process:

1. Preheat the griddle to medium-high heat.
2. Toss sweet potatoes with oil, Chili pepper, and common salt/sea salt. Place sweet potato wedges on a hot griddle and cook over medium heat for 6 mins.
3. Flip and cook for 6-8 mins more.
4. Serve and enjoy!

Nutrition Values: Cals: 263 Fat: 12g Carbs: 35g Proteins: 4g

Spiced Chickpeas

Ingredients Needed:

◊ 1 (16-oz) can of chickpeas, drained
◊ ¼ cup of olive oil
◊ 1 -tbsp full of ground cumin
◊ 1 -tbsp full of smoked paprika
◊ 1 -tsp full of garlic powder
◊ 1 -tsp full of onion powder
◊ 1 -tsp full of kosher common salt/ sea salt, + more to taste

PREPARATION:
5 MINS

COOKING TIME:
30 MINS

SERVING PORTIONS:
2

Preparation Process:

1. Combine all ingredients in a large mixing bowl. Pour the mixture onto a cool griddle grill and bring the griddle to medium heat.
2. Allow the mixture to slowly come to temperature and continue to cook, frequently stirring for up to 30 mins until the garbanzo beans become crispy and crunchy.
3. Serve and enjoy!

Nutrition Values: Cals: 180 Fat: 7g Carbs: 26g Proteins: 6g

Guacamole Bruschetta

Ingredients Needed:

◊ 8 oz baguette bread, cut into 1-inch slices
◊ 2 -tbsp full of olive oil

FOR THE TOPPING:

◊ 2 avocados, well diced
◊ 1 -tsp full of lemon juice
◊ 1 -tsp full of garlic, well minced
◊ ¼ -tsp of Chili pepper
◊ ¼ -tsp of common salt/sea salt

PREPARATION:
10 MINS

COOKING TIME:
5 MINS

SERVING PORTIONS:
8

Preparation Process:

1. Preheat the griddle to high heat.
2. Brush your bread slices with oil and place on a hot griddle top and cook until lightly golden brown from both sides.
3. In your mixing bowl, add all topping ingredients and mix well. Spoon the topping mixture over the bread slices.
4. Serve.

Nutrition Values: Cals: 100 Fat: 9g Carbs: 5g Proteins: 1g

Cauliflower Bites

Ingredients Needed:

◊ 1 lb. cauliflower florets
◊ 1 -tsp full of ground coriander
◊ 1/2 -tsp of dried rosemary
◊ 1 and 1/2 -tsp of garlic powder
◊ 1 -tbsp full of olive oil
◊ 1 -tsp full of sesame seeds
◊ Common salt/sea salt and Chili pepper to taste

PREPARATION:
5 MINS

COOKING TIME:
10 MINS

SERVING PORTIONS:
4

Preparation Process:

1. Preheat the griddle to high heat and use frying spray to coat the griddle's top.
2. Add cauliflower florets and remaining ingredients into the mixing bowl, toss well, and spread on the hot griddle top.
3. Cook cauliflower florets until tender.
4. Serve and enjoy!

Nutrition Values: Cals: 65 Fat 4g Carbs: 7.1g Proteins: 2.6g

Buttered Popcorn

Ingredients Needed:

◊ 3 -tbsp full of peanut oil
◊ ½ cup of popcorn kernels
◊ 3 -tbsp full of butter
◊ Common salt/sea salt to taste

PREPARATION:
5 MINS

COOKING TIME:
4 MINS

SERVING PORTIONS:
2 - 4

Preparation Process:

1. Heat the griddle grill to medium-high heat and add the peanut oil. While it is heating place 5 popcorn kernels in the oil.
2. When 2 or 3 pop, add the butter to the oil and pour in the remaining kernels. Cover immediately with a tall pan or spaghetti pot.
3. When the popcorn starts popping stir to get all the kernels to pop and prevent the popped corn from burning.
4. Using insulated gloves, toss the popcorn by moving the pan or pot from side to side on the griddle without lifting.
5. Cook for about 4 mins until the popping slows down to once every few seconds.
6. Serve with common salt/sea salt and enjoy!

Nutrition Values: Cals: 78 Fat: 5g Carbs: 7g Proteins: 1g

Figs with Walnuts and Honey

Ingredients Needed:

◊ 8 ripe figs, stemmed
◊ 2 -tbsp full of walnut oil
◊ 8 walnut halves, toasted
◊ ¼ cup of honey

**PREPARATION:
10 MINS**

**COOKING TIME:
10 MINS**

**SERVING
PORTIONS:
4**

Preparation Process:

1. Brush the figs with the walnut oil, then cut an x in the stem ends. Push 1 walnut ½ into each fig.
2. Grease the cooking surface of the griddle with cooking oil and preheat the griddle to medium heat.
3. Put the figs on the griddle grate, stem side up, and then let it cook until the fruit softens, 5 to 10 mins.
4. Transfer to a platter, drizzle with the honey and serve!

Nutrition Values: Cals: 304 Fat 14.9g Carbs: 12g Proteins: 21g

Fruit Pound Cake

Ingredients Needed:

◊ 6 slices of pound cake
◊ 3 peaches, well cut and pitted
◊ 3 bananas, peeled and well cut
◊ 24 strawberries, large
◊ ½ cup of simple syrup
◊ Raspberry sauce to taste
◊ Whipped cream to taste
◊ Mint leaves for garnishing

PREPARATION:
10 MINS

COOKING TIME:
10 MINS

SERVING PORTIONS:
6

Preparation Process:

1. Grease the cooking surface of the griddle using frying spray to coat the griddle's top and preheat to medium heat.
2. Arrange the pound cake, bananas, peaches, and strawberries on the griddle. Cook on both sides to your desired doneness.
3. Toss the fruit with simple syrup and transfer it to your serving plate.
4. Top with raspberry sauce and whipped cream as you like.
5. Garnish with mint leaves and serve.

Nutrition Values: Cals: 338 Fat 12g Carbs: 14g Proteins: 27g

Apricots with Brioche

Ingredients Needed:

◊ 2 cups of vanilla ice cream
◊ 2 -tbsp full of honey
◊ 4 slices brioches, well diced
◊ 2 -tbsp full of sugar
◊ 2 -tbsp full of butter
◊ 8 ripe apricots

PREPARATION:
10 MINS

COOKING TIME:
4 – 5 MINS

SERVING PORTIONS:
4

Preparation Process:

1. Mix the halved apricots with sugar and butter.
2. Grease the cooking surface of the griddle using frying spray to coat the griddle's top and preheat to medium heat.
3. Put the brioche slices onto the griddle for 1 minute per side. Grill your apricots in the griddle for 1 minute per side.
4. Top the brioche slices with honey, apricot slices, and a scoop of vanilla ice cream.
5. Serve and enjoy!

Nutrition Values: Cals: 212 Fat: 9g Carbs: 28g Proteins: 4g

Caramelized 5-Spice Oranges

Ingredients Needed:

◊ ¼ cup of sugar
◊ ½ -tsp full of five-spice powder
◊ 2 large oranges
◊ ¼ cup of well minced fresh mint

PREPARATION:
5 MINS

COOKING TIME:
15 MINS

SERVING PORTIONS:
4

Preparation Process:

1. Grease the cooking surface of the griddle using frying spray to coat the griddle's top and preheat to medium heat.
2. Stir the sugar and five-spice powder together on a small plate.
3. Slice a sliver off the top and bottom of each of your oranges. Remove any seeds and press the cut side of each ½ into the sugar. Put the orange halves on the griddle, sugared side up, and then let it cook for 6 to 8 mins.
4. Turn them over and then let them cook until the cut sides brown, 2 to 3 mins.
5. Transfer them to your serving plates and sprinkle them with the mint.
6. Serve and enjoy!

Nutrition Values: Cals: 397 Fat 21g Carbs: 8g Proteins: 22g

Berry Cobbler

Ingredients Needed:

◊ 2 cans (21-oz) pie filling raspberry flavor
◊ Vanilla ice cream, as you like
◊ 1 (8-ounces) package of cake mix
◊ ½ cup of olive oil
◊ 1 and ¼ cups of water

PREPARATION:
10 MINS

COOKING TIME:
20 MINS

SERVING PORTIONS:
2

Preparation Process:

1. Grease the cooking surface of the griddle using frying spray to coat the griddle's top and preheat to medium heat.
2. Mix your cake mix with olive oil and water in a suitable mixing bowl until smooth. Place a foil packet on the working surface along with the pie filling.
3. Spread your cake mix on top of the pie filling.
4. Cover your foil packet, seal it, and cook on the griddle until set.
5. Serve and enjoy!

Nutrition Values: Cals: 319 Fat: 11.9g Carbs: 14.8g Proteins: 5g

Conclusion

Now that you have all the information you require and have learned how to make the most of your griddle, you just have to turn it on and start cooking delicious foods with it. Indulge yourself and make meals that your visitors, family or friends will genuinely appreciate!

You could help other people use their griddle to the fullest extent by giving a review if you liked this guide. Your feedback is very important to me.

I sincerely appreciate you taking the time to read this cookbook and I wish you the best.

Made in the USA
Monee, IL
28 June 2023